QUILTSKILLS

NOV   1999

DEMCO

WORKSHOPS
FROM

QUILTSKILLS

THE
QUILTERS'
GUILD
AUSTRALIA

CONTENTS

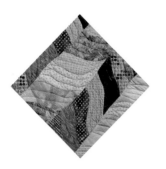

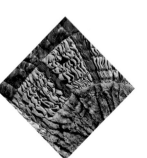

The Quilters' Guild gratefully acknowledges the following:

J.B. Fairfax Press Pty Limited for their continued support of the work of the Guild;

Margaret Rolfe for her foreword; the eleven Quilters' Guild tutors for their

acceptance of the challenge; and the members of the organising committee — Carolyn Sullivan

(Chairman), Lynden Abbott, Karen Fail, Lynn Hewitt and Daphne Massie.

INTRODUCTION

It seems timely that The Quilters' Guild, with its wealth of talented quiltmakers who spend much of their quiltmaking year sharing their expertise with others, should publish some of this body of work. It is hoped that this will enable even more quilt lovers to have the opportunity to learn from them.

The challenge of this book to the tutors was to take their students beyond basic patchwork and quilting, and extend their design skills and technical expertise. This has certainly been achieved by the eleven tutors featured. They have surpassed all expectations and provided some challenging ideas for all quilters, whether beginners or the more experienced. Not only can you follow the instructions, but you can extend your thinking way beyond and create wonderful designs of your own. The aim of this book is to challenge you, as the tutors have been challenged.

Learning is an important part of our lives. We spend all our childhood working on it! This prepares us for the skills we wish to pursue as adults. All quiltmakers are constantly searching for new ways of creating their masterpieces. It is the role of The Quilters' Guild to provide avenues and opportunities for its members on their journey of discovery.

This book should certainly achieve that goal.

Carolyn Sullivan
President 1995-96

THE CHALLENGE OF CREATIVITY

On reading through these workshops, I found a single thread ran through them: creativity. This should not have surprised me, as I know that the teachers of these workshops comprise some of Australia's most talented and creative quiltmakers. These are the quilters whose quilts you see in books and in the top Australian and international exhibitions. Their knowledge, technical expertise and quiltmaking experience is second to none.

These people are recognised as being creative, but what does that mean to the rest of us, who may consider ourselves to be less blessed with creativity?

To create means to bring something into being. It means that something is made that was not there before. That is the scary bit — people find it hard to imagine that it is possible for them, as ordinary mortals, to make something that is new and did not exist before. The mind goes blank, the page is empty and the black box is a void. We are inclined to believe that creation belongs only to the chosen few, a gift which we have not been given.

But is this true? I would like to challenge the idea that creativity is a state of being and, moreover, that it is either given or not given, like a light switch which is either on or off. I want to suggest that creativity is a journey, not a state. It is a process, not a product.

If creativity is a journey, it is clear that you have to start somewhere and move along in a direction. If you think about creativity in this way, it becomes much less scary. To be on a journey, you just have to begin where you are, and make a step. The journey continues as step after step is made. What happens with creativity, you will find, is that one discovery will lead to another discovery, then another and another and another. This is how the process of discovery works. It is taking the first step which is important.

If you think of creativity as a journey, you can also understand that the journey may well have been taken by people before you, so that there are those who are on a similar journey, but who are further down the track. These are the people who can help us, whose experience we can use to illuminate our own path. Not that other people have answers for us — the creative journey is one that, in the end, is taken alone. Would you expect to learn the piano by reading a book about how to play the piano? No, you know that mastering an instrument takes hours, days, years of practice to hone the skills, learn techniques and improve the performance. But you would look to teachers for help and guidance: to set you exercises, suggest directions and give you pointers from their own experience.

So it is with these workshops. They can be used as a step – even a first step – on a journey of creativity. It is not necessarily that you want to create what they have created, but rather that, by doing a workshop, you will learn, grow and experience. The mastering of a new technique may suggest an idea, or an idea might demand that we learn new techniques in order to express it. The more we experience, the more resources we have to draw on, the more those fleeting moments of inspiration can move into a state of being. Creation, in fact.

From suggestions on design and methods of collage to techniques of fabric manipulation, from procedures for special effects in fabric dyeing to the processes involved in piecing personal ideas, from methods of machine-appliqué to investigations of curved piecing, and from the construction of cubes and compasses to the use of crazy patchwork in new and pictorial ways – this book offers much for you to experience and grow on. This book exists to encourage you to expand your creativity.

Go on! Take a step!

Margaret Rolfe

FIRE OF THE NEVER NEVER
27¹/₂ in x 34¹/₄ in (70 cm x 87 cm)

COLLAGE FOR ART QUILTS

A Workshop in Textiles and Design

SUE WADEMAN

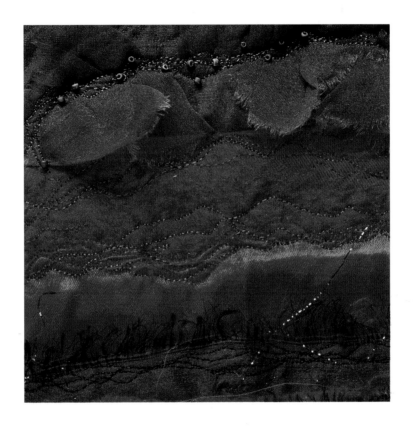

The uniquely Australian outback landscape with its vast, open spaces and vibrant colours has been the inspiration for my latest art quilts. As a young child, I wanted very much to be an artist. Now, with the graphic design skills acquired in the commercial art field and the knowledge of textiles developed as a quiltmaker, I can truly say that I am a passionate textile artist.

This workshop will challenge and stimulate both the beginner and the experienced quiltmaker; in fact, anyone who is ready to experience a whole new way of working with fabrics. It is not a workshop in precision piecing or detailed appliqué, but rather an invitation to free up the usual way of creating patch-work, using patterns and only cotton fabrics. I hope you will be encouraged to create your own designs, using all types of fabrics as your palette.

The *Macquarie Dictionary* defines collage as 'a pictorial composition, made from a combination of various materials, affixed in juxtaposition to a surface, and often combined with colour and line from the artist's own hand'. We are the artists, the colours are our fabrics and the line is created by our stitchery and quilting.

Collage with textiles is the technique I use for my own art quilts and teach to my students. It is a method which encourages more spontaneity and a more intuitive use of fabric.

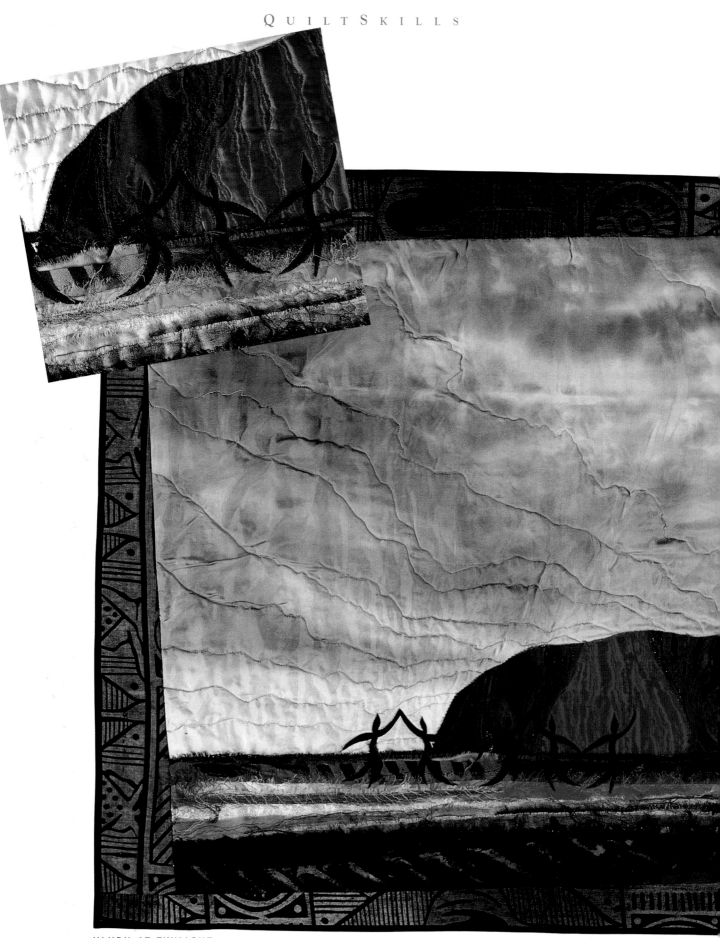

ULURU AT TWILIGHT
34 in x 61 in (86 cm x 155 cm)

Exercise 1 – Line

COLLECTING YOUR PALETTE

An artist can't work without a full colour palette and a textile artist can't work without a large variety of fabrics. You will need to collect lots of different sheer fabrics in as many colours as possible. This group of fabrics includes polyesters, nylon, chiffon and, my favourite, silk organza. Silk organza is the most transparent of all and it also frays wonderfully.

Scraps of hand-dyed silks are very useful; dye your own or find someone who does. For texture, raw silks are great, especially the ones that fray, revealing a different colour on the two edges. Embossed blends, satin, taffeta, lace, burlap and cheesecloth are all important to include. Netting and fine tulle are great for overlays; metallics and acetates add sparkle – the variety is endless.

Interesting fabrics can be found in many unexpected places:

- dressmakers' rubbish bins – they throw away fabric scraps that textile artists can use;
- leftovers from bridal gown boutiques and costume-making workrooms;
- fabric samples – some of these are never seen on rolls;
- remnant bins in dress fabric shops;
- shops and markets for secondhand clothes;
- discontinued swatches from curtain makers and interior decorators; and
- the floor after a Collage for Art Quilts workshop is often a good source!

Of course, you can also purchase small pieces of interesting textiles available in stores in the most wonderful array of colours.

Once you have collected your palette, sort it by colour. I use large see-through plastic bags for the bigger pieces and see-through plastic jars for the smaller ones.

SOURCES AND REFERENCE MATERIALS

Design ideas are everywhere in the natural and in the man-made environment. If you haven't yet started collecting pictures for your reference file, then start now with magazines, travel brochures, postcards, greeting cards, leaflets, art magazines, interior design catalogues, to name just a few. Take photos wherever you go. Learn to actually see what is around you – don't just look.

Get up close and find the detail, patterns and amazing designs in nature. The Australian landscape has been the inspiration for many of my quilts. The intensity of the colours is unique. Learn to observe the landscape closely and you will have an endless source of design ideas.

DESIGN EXERCISES

The fundamental ingredient for a great quilt is a great design. Following are five exercises based on the elements of design: line, shape, value, texture and colour. For each exercise, I have specified some limits, because it is often as you limit the choices that the design improves. As the saying goes: 'Necessity is the mother of invention'.

WHAT YOU NEED

Lots and lots of different fabrics

1⅛ yd (1 m) of a neutral, plain homespun or calico

1⅛ yd (1 m) of fusible webbing

Iron and a protective ironing mat

Cardboard

Rotary cutter, quilter's ruler and cutting mat

2B pencil and ruler

Masking tape

Rayon embroidery thread to match the fabrics

Metallic and some heavier threads (if your machine will take them)

Beads and ribbons

Sewing machine in good working order with a free-motion embroidery foot and a normal foot

Usual sewing supplies: needles, pins, scissors etc

Hand cream to keep your fingers soft and sensitive while arranging the collage

PREPARATION

Cut two pieces of cardboard: one a little larger than 8½ in x 11 in (21.5 cm x 28 cm) and one 8½ in x 11 in (21.5 cm x 28 cm) with a 6 in x 9 in (15 cm x 23 cm) hole cut in the centre. This second one will act as a mount through which to view your collage.

Prewash and press the homespun or calico, then cut five pieces, each 8 in x 12 in (20 cm x 30 cm), one for each of the five exercises. On each piece, draw a pencil line 1½ in (4 cm) from each edge, then cut a piece of fusible webbing to the size of this drawn rectangle. Iron it onto the centre of the fabric, rough side down. Do not peel off the paper backing until you are ready to start each exercise, then peel it off, leaving the 'glue' on the fabric surface. Place the piece of fabric, glue side up, on the larger piece of cardboard. This will prevent the fabric from sticking to itself and will make it easier to carry your work in progress to and from the ironing board without disturbing it.

EXERCISE 1 – LINE

Lines can be thick or thin, straight or curved, parallel or converging.

For this exercise the limits are that the lines must travel in one direction, be fairly straight and vary randomly from thick (approximately ¾ in (2 cm)) to thin (just a sliver showing). Limit your choices to warm colours, such as yellow, orange, red, maroon, pink etc, and, within this range, limit the colour choice even more to include just a few of these.

With the prepared backing fabric and your selected fabric palette in front of you, begin to cut, tear or find random strips to place horizontally or vertically across the glued area. Allow them to overlap, but some part of them must touch the glue. Work fairly quickly until the area is completely covered and you are pleased with your design. Place the mount over your work and view it through the frame. This masking of the edges gives you a better idea of how your design is progressing. Add extra pieces or take some out, as the fabric 'speaks' to you.

When you are happy with the design, put the ironing mat or the paper backing off the fusible webbing over it. Carry it to the ironing board, with the cardboard underneath. Carefully slip the cardboard out from under it and press the design with the iron. If some pieces are not quite attached, they can be caught later with the stitching.

For the stitchery, make sure the threads you choose blend with the colours of the fabrics. Stitch, following the fabric edges, or free-machine stitch, drawing in lines to further enhance the design.

This same exercise can also be done with diagonal lines which give an energetic feeling of movement to a piece of work. Use them to advantage.

Exercise 2 – Shape

EXERCISE 2 – SHAPE

Shape is the form a line produces. It can be geometric or freeflowing, large or small, overlapping or freestanding. It is the organisation and repetition of shapes that give a design balance and make an interesting composition. In a still-life work, the design is often given depth by overlapping the different shapes, and a sense of balance by repeating some similar ones. The shapes near the edge can be cut off by the frame which gives the viewer a sense of involvement in the piece.

For this exercise, the limit is that you choose only one shape – it can be geometric or organic. The shapes must overlap and be of varying sizes. This time, limit yourself to a cool colour scheme of blues, greens, teals, purples etc.

Begin by cutting lots of your chosen shape, repeating the same sizes several times. Place them down, overlapping, and making sure that some part of each shape touches the glue.

View your work through the cardboard mount to check if you have balanced the design, then cover it and iron the pieces in place. Again, if all the pieces are not caught, they can easily be stitched down later.

For the stitching, this time use some matching metallic threads and stitch around the shapes, but do not follow the edge too closely. Add a few fancy stitches for additional interest, if you wish.

EXERCISE 3 – VALUE

Value is the lightness or darkness of a colour. It creates the depth and mood of a design. We often talk about the value of a fabric where we require a shading effect. The effect given by these value changes is well demonstrated in my quilt 'Uluru at Twilight'. The gradated sky, hand-dyed by Jan Taylor, gives this quilt an amazing illusion of depth and sets the mood for the whole image.

You will need to have sheer fabrics in your palette for this exercise and, although they can be used in the other exercises, this is where these see-through fabrics come into their own.

For this exercise, limit yourself to just one colour, and extend it through the value range. For example, if you choose a cerise pink, then take it darker towards maroon and lighter towards the pastel pinks. Use the darks at the bottom and gradate them up to the lights at the top.

View the design through the mount, then cover and iron it as for the others. Take particular care when ironing synthetics – do not use a hot iron.

EXERCISE 4 – TEXTURE

Texture is the roughness or smoothness of any particular material.

The textile artist has a unique opportunity to use this element of design to its best advantage. Creating with linen, burlap, embossed-type blends, raw silk, woven wool, lace, netting and so on gives the work a tactile appeal not easily achieved by other art forms.

Use textured fabrics to advantage in this exercise by choosing an organic shape and only one colour

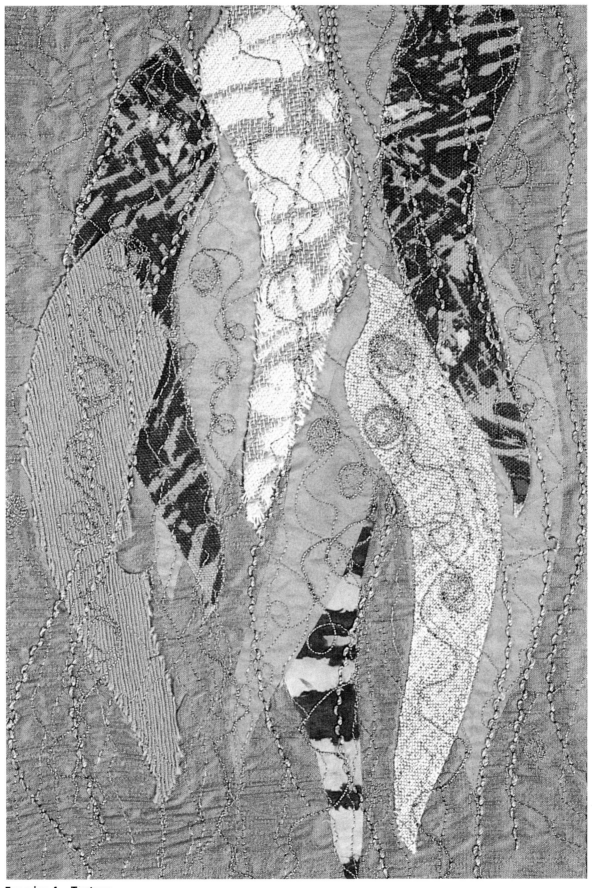

Exercise 4 – Texture

Exercise 5 – Colour

(all of its values) and as many different-textured fabrics as you can.

Remember to overlap the shapes and repeat them to make an interesting composition.

When the design is fused to the backing, add more texture with the bobbin-worked threads as shown in the sample on page 17.

EXERCISE 5 – COLOUR

Colour is detected by our eyes when light is reflected off an object. I could talk at length about colour theory, but I feel it is sufficient to say that colour gives life to everything. It is the essence of any art work. Colour is the visual impact of the quilt. It is what captures the viewer's initial interest and holds their attention. Colour gives your work life and holds the expressive quality of the artist's intent. I

describe myself as a Colourist, for colour is my passion, and very often the source of inspiration for a quilt. The reds in the 'Fire of the Never Never' express the uniqueness of the outback landscape. The different shades of red create the feeling of the heat and vastness of the desert.

Choose a simple line format and two contrasting colours – one warm and one cool. Experiment with different ratios of the two colours to see how the feel of the design changes.

EXTENSION EXERCISE

Now that you have thought about and experienced the elements of design – line, shape, value, texture and colour, it is time to put your new-found skills and ideas to work in your own landscape or still-life picture. A vase of flowers is a good place to start.

Find your reference material and choose your colour palette. Start with the background, then using the many different textiles in your collection, build up the layers of leaves and stems, putting the flower shapes on last. This piece could be incorporated into a quilt or framed.

Remember, design ideas are everywhere. Hold on to your vision, work intuitively, trust yourself, be brave … and let go!

STILL LIFE WITH FLOWERS

WATERWEAVE
37¹/₂ in x 43 in (95 cm x 110 cm)

IRREGULAR-
SHAPED QUILTS

ALISON SCHWABE

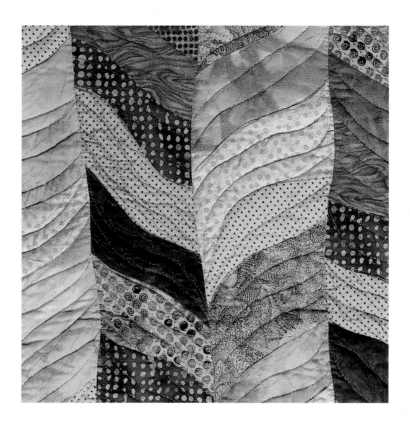

Since the late 1970s, thousands of Australians of all ages, mostly women, but many children and some men, have gained great pleasure and satisfaction from the expanding craft of quiltmaking. Skills and techniques are taught in classes and workshops run by fabric shops, quilting associations and community organisations. Many publications produce patterns for quilters' projects, generally based on the popular traditional British and American quilt designs. But Australians have also developed some unique styles, including waggas, embroidered coverlets and lively contemporary art quilts.

It is characteristically human to follow tradition – and equally human to stray from it. Historically, a close connection existed between the shape of a quilted piece and its purpose – principally bedding or clothing. Today, an irregular-shaped bed or a particular-shaped alcove or wall may occasionally tempt a quilt designer to break out of the safe four straight sides and four right angles, but we rarely see a round, hexagonal or other unusual shape. In many of today's popular wall quilts, beautifully made fish will swim underwater in a square or rectangle, birds fly against a rectangular sky, or some clever geometric shape will be set against a plain square.

Comparatively few quiltmakers totally design their own work, but many more carry out changes, adapting traditional or published patterns to their own ends. To really connect design content to shape raises a number of questions:

■ What shape does this design suggest/demand?

■ What about a border?

■ How could I finish such an edge?

■ Would this treatment be relevant to the overall design?

■ What difference might this make to the hanging arrangements?

■ What about the 10 cm (4 in) sleeve usually asked for?

Any of these and other problems can overwhelm and persuade the designer to produce another square, rectangle – or even a UFO (unfinished object)! I feel more of us might make more daring departures into the 'Original Design Zone' if we had the confidence to deal with some of the unusual and irregular-shaped problems we risk finding.

In my work, I favour the repeat block format, the American influence. Places I have lived or travelled in, I associate with particular colours, and the non-traditional block shapes are influenced by patterns within that particular landscape. The result may not even be a block, as such, but may become a repeated unit. In 'Mission Beach', for example, graded bands of colour change within an overall shape suggested by a breaking wave. My quilts are originally designed as pieces of wall art and, although I do make a bed-sized quilt from time to time, most of my pieces are in the 30 in–60 in (0.75–1.5 m) size range, intended for use in decoration of homes, offices and other buildings. As they essentially compete in the market-place with other two-dimensional artforms, including paintings, drawings and prints, I prefer to show my work in multimedia art gallery shows or in contemporary quilt shows.

Standard shapes and sizes determine the design of most bed quilts. But wall quilts can be free of size and shape restraints; edge treatments can range from minimal to elaborate; and there are several ways of hanging them. The irregular-shaped quilts I have made have been in response to a need for the shape to enhance the design concept, and partly as a response to the absence of rules governing personal statements in quiltmaking.

For your own expressions in contemporary quilt-making, you'll find ideas in this chapter, offering much scope for experimentation with a dash of imagination. Good craftsmanship is always important, but no matter how fine your needlework skills, some of these non-traditional techniques may not be as well appreciated as you would like, if you enter them in judged traditional quilt shows.

MAKING AN IRREGULAR-SHAPED QUILT

As can be seen in the photograph on page 20, the design consists of irregular-shaped repeated 'blocks' in vertical bands of light and dark fabrics, forming peaks on the irregular-shaped upper and lower edges. These bands of units are sewn together in gently curved shapes.

REQUIREMENTS

For a piece about 1⅛ yd (1 m) square finished, you will need at least fourteen pieces of fabric, each about 10 in (25 cm). This project is great for scrap pieces as each unit is only small. Theoretically, you could have every shape in a different print, but repetition of shape, colour and print/texture increases harmony in the design, so I would recommend fourteen to twenty different fabrics. For a larger size quilt, have more fabric to hand and, of course, the quilt could be made as a miniature, too. It is impossible to be precise, as the pattern is so flexible, so you

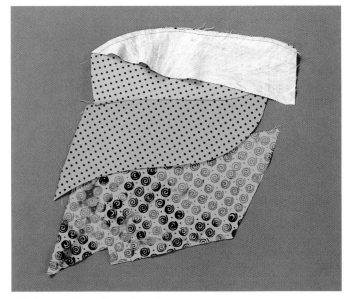

Joining units to form bands

MISSION BEACH
48 in x 50 in
(122 cm x 127 cm)

must decide your own size requirements. And what to do with the scraps is the subject of a whole other workshop!

MAKE A WORKING PLAN AND A SAMPLE
It is a good idea to draw up a working plan or mock-up of a quilt. For my quilt, the plan features repeated leaf-shaped units joined in vertical strips. These strips are then joined along gently curved seams to form the shape, featuring curved peaks on the top and bottom edges. As you draw up your plan, include notes of choices regarding fabric, size and surface

design techniques, such as patchwork, appliqué, painting, hand- or machine-embroidery and quilting techniques. Consider the need for reinforcement, and possible hanging and edge treatments. Record your alternatives and final choices on your plan.

Before working on your full-sized piece, it's a good idea to make a sample on which you can test whether your edge treatment will work on the various shapes and stiffenings. Sew a plain front piece, batting and backing together to make a potholder-sized test piece. Later, a loop can be added and even your sample becomes a decorative and useful piece.

CONSTRUCTION

This quilt uses a template-free rotary-cut construction method. If you haven't previously tried these techniques, carefully work through the process as an exercise before starting on your quilt.

The sample photographed on page 22 shows the joining of the units to form the vertical bands. Joining the units and the bands uses the following cutting and construction principles:

■ Place both fabrics right side up, then rotary cut a curved line through both fabrics at the same time (Fig. 1). Keep the curve very gentle to begin with; with experience, you can become braver with more curve in the line.

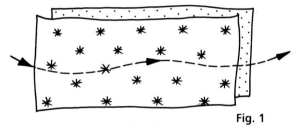

Fig. 1

■ Place the fabrics from the opposite sides of the cut edge-to-edge. They will fit together (Fig. 2).

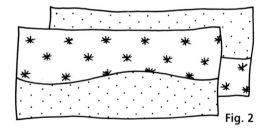

Fig. 2

■ Make chalk hatches across the cut line or pencil dots on either side of it, as an aid to matching (Fig. 3). With the right sides facing, pin the two pieces together along the cut edge and sew a narrow seam (only $3/16$ in (3 mm)). Press the seam to one side. If you have followed the steps carefully, the seam will lie flat with no bumps and no need to clip and notch the curves.

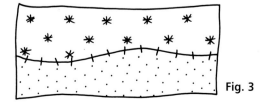

Fig. 3

When you are comfortable with the technique, it's time to construct the vertical bands. Begin by cutting shape A1 from a piece of fabric approximately $8^5/8$ in (22 cm) square (Fig. 4). Lay A1 on the next piece of fabric that is approximately 8–10 in (20–25 cm) wide and using the Edge 1/2 as a cutting guide, cut out A2 as shown (Fig. 5). Repeat these steps until you have cut a vertical band that is approximately 49 in (125 cm) long (or your desired length). Stitch the band together. Ignore the irregular or wobbly edges at this stage.

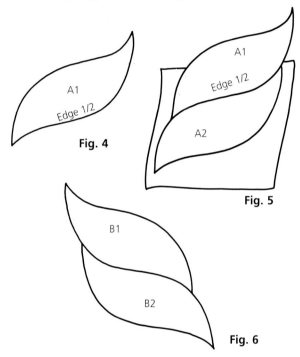

Fig. 4

Fig. 5

Fig. 6

Make Band B in the same way, but reversing the direction of the shape (Fig. 6). Make Band C the same as Band A, and Band D the same as Band B, and so on.

Trim both sides of Band A as shown in figure 7, then lay the trimmed edge of Band A over the edge of Band B and cut and join as for the earlier instruction on rotary-cut curved piecing (Fig. 8).

EMBELLISHMENT

After I finished piecing this quilt, I embroidered the top with matching metallic threads, echoing the shapes. Set the machine on a long setting of the five-point zigzag, giving a wavy line, and thread it with metallic sewing machine threads. Explore your own machine for its embroidery potential. Add the beading or hand-embroidery only after finishing the edge.

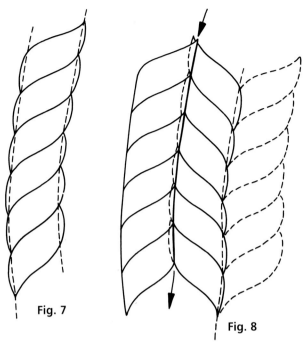

Fig. 7

Fig. 8

the sewing machine, I used free machine-quilting to echo the leaf shapes, and also quilted in the ditch of the seams that join the bands, using monofilament thread for this step.

REINFORCEMENT

'Waterweave' had 'pointy bits' at the top edge which would eventually flop forward, so a stiffening was cut then sewn between the backing and batting (Fig. 9). If you are making an envelope-style backing, add the stiffening later (Fig. 10). For the stiffening use template plastic, plastic from a margarine container, buckram or canvas and cut it small enough to prevent it being caught in the seam allowance – otherwise the facing edge will never flatten nicely. Slip the stiffening between the backing and the batting and quilt through it in a few places to secure it.

QUILTING

Cut the batting and backing, each approximately 1–2 in (2.5–5 cm) larger all round than the shape of the top. I quilted 'Waterweave' using a walking foot with the machine set on topstitch. If your machine doesn't have a topstitch setting, use a slightly longer than usual stitch. I used matching machine-sewing thread in the bobbin and Prism by Madeira for the top thread. This is easy to work with, as long as you loosen the top tension, use a larger needle (size 100 or a jeans needle) and sew slowly. A medium-loft wool batting, available off the roll, works well for hand- or machine-quilting. Using the walking foot on

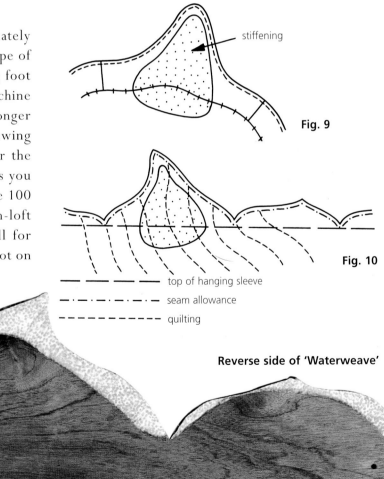

stiffening

Fig. 9

Fig. 10

– – – – top of hanging sleeve

– · – · – seam allowance

– – – – quilting

Reverse side of 'Waterweave'

If you are quilting by machine, baste and do a test to make sure that your machine will sew through the stiffening. My machine sewed through template plastic quite well. Just go carefully, ignore the 'pop-pop' noise and allow it to feed through as evenly as possible. If this is beyond your machine, use a very stiff, woven stiffening, such as buckram or canvas.

For the envelope-style backing, add the stiffening with the quilting or attach it with a few holding stitches after quilting, but before adding the backing.

EDGE TREATMENTS

The edge of 'Waterweave' is faced, just like the neck or armhole edges of a garment. With the right sides together, sew a 1¼ in (3 cm) wide strip to the front of the quilt, turn it to the back, gently pressed or anti-roll stitched, then hand-stitch it into place.

On curves and peaks, the facing is cut to shape and seams are clipped and notched to allow the seam to lie flat when it is turned back. 'Pointy bits' are also faced by a piece cut to shape, anti-roll stitched (it's really worth doing) and hand-stitched to the back of the quilt (Fig. 11). Several alternative edge treatments are dealt with later, all offering great potential to deal with any shape you want.

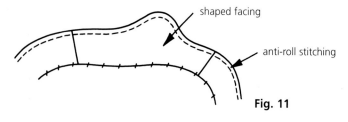

shaped facing

anti-roll stitching

Fig. 11

HANGING

For 'Waterweave' I cut plywood to the approximate shape (using a jigsaw), sandpapered it smooth, sprayed it with some clear sealer, and drilled a couple of holes in it so it could be secured to the wall. I attached Velcro strips in suitable places to

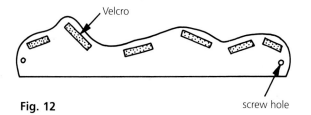

Velcro

Fig. 12   screw hole

match those sewn to the back of the quilt (Fig. 12). Consider this method for miniatures too.

FURTHER OPTIONS

Construction The curved piecing and edging techniques can be used in a wide variety of shapes, limited only by your imagination. It is also possible to construct this design using a cartoon, and cutting individual pattern shapes. You can also get a similar effect if you cut and apply the shapes to a base fabric in crazy quilt style of construction.

Embellishment Although machine-embroidery needs to be done before quilting and finishing, further embellishments of hand-embroidery, beading, couched threads, the attachment of found objects – such as shells, 'seaweedy' kinds of ribbons etc – can all be added after the finishing steps.

Quilting The quilt can be quilted by hand or by machine, or a combination of both. You can make your quilting an eye-catching feature of the surface decoration or it can be purely constructional in function and invisible, for example, if it is 'in the ditch'. There are so many different threads you could use, all with different needle requirements. Explore what might be possible with your hands or your machine.

Edge treatments Traditional quilts usually have single or multiple borders plus binding, which define and finish off the edge. These can also be used on non-traditional quilts, of course, but as shapes change, these techniques can become difficult, even impossible, to use. If so, try one of the following alternatives for finishing the edges.

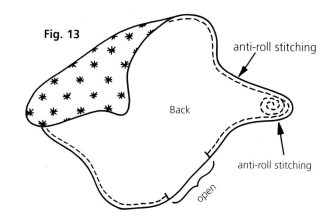

Fig. 13

anti-roll stitching

Back

anti-roll stitching

open

Envelope-style backing is a particularly useful finish for a piece to be attached to the front of another piece. Complete all the quilting and surface stitchery, then cut the backing exactly the same size and shape as the front. Any stiffening is attached by hand or machine before the backing is added. Sew the backing to the front with the right sides together, leaving 4–6 in (10–15 cm) unstitched, so the whole thing can be turned right side out. Hand-stitch the opening closed. If the seam rolls forward a little, do anti-roll stitchery on the back or some constructional quilting to hold the seam flat (Fig. 13). Add extra anti-roll stitching in the shaped areas.

Satin stitch by machine or over-locker/serger provides a minimal but firm finish. With no shape limitations, this technique offers great possibilities. Complete all the surface decoration and quilting, then sew a line of machine stay stitching around the raw edge in a matching thread. Trim the edge to about $3/16$ in (3 mm), then satin stitch close enough to cover the stay stitching and bind the raw edge.

Choose thread for its potential – glittery lamé, shiny richly coloured rayon, or something that blends with the fabric. If you want the edge to lie flat, take care it does not stretch; but you can get a beautifully buckled edge by stretching the edge as you sew. Consider the colour of your backing and bobbin thread. If you want a metallic binding, closely satin stitch the edge first with a matching thread, then oversew with your metallic zigzag. These stitches offer a slightly less effective coverage, but the edge will already have been effectively bound by the first row of satin stitches. Your overlocker, of course, does the whole thing in one operation. Experiment with a variety of different threads and stitch combinations.

Cut and frayed edges are very effective. After quilting, run a line of stay stitching around the raw edged shape, then trim the edge to within $3/16$ in–$1/4$ in (4–5 mm) of the stitch line with no further finishing done. Or, you could do several lines of stitchery, and again, the choice of thread and colour is yours, according to what effect you want. With a wider seam allowance, the batting layer could be trimmed so it does not show, but here you may want it to show; it could also be painted or dyed. Tease the edges out with a needle or wire brush, or pop the quilt into the dryer to whizz around for a while; or put it into the washing machine before the dryer – the edges will be well frayed. Coarse-woven fabrics fray more easily. Experiment first on a sample, unless you are brave and don't mind what happens.

SLEEVES

Hanging a straight and gently shaped quilt is simple with a traditional sleeve 4–4$3/4$ in (10–12 cm) wide, or several sleeves, on the back. Make sure neither the sleeve nor the rod will show from the front. Regardless of material composition, visible rods detract much more than they add to the overall effect of any design. For a breezy place, you may need to add a sleeve and rod along the bottom to add enough weight to steady it, or it too can be fastened to the wall. If the wall surface is suitable, Velcro dots are sufficient to hang miniatures or small quilts. If you have a suitable stairwell or alcove, consider suspending the piece by means of fine fishing line and tiny metal loops, so that it seems to float in the space.

COLOURS OF THE DAY
45¹/₄ in x 55 in (115 cm x 140 cm)

JOURNEY OF A THOUSAND MILES

WENDY SACLIER

The title of this workshop is intended to reflect the unending journey in crazy patchwork — only the quilter can determine when and where to stop.

I was first introduced to patchwork and quilting in 1976 by Margaret Rolfe and Judy Thompson, both of whom had lived in the United States and had returned to Australia with a new interest to share. Caught up in their enthusiasm, I began a journey that I am still travelling.

The last twenty years has seen many changes in direction in quiltmaking, in general and for me personally. For fourteen years, I made quilts with my mother, Vivienne Mildren, sharing our love of hand-embroidery and quilts.

These days, inspirations for new quilts flow in from a variety of sources and I look forward to developing these ideas as the shelves full of fabric beckon me. I look forward to the time when I will be able to quilt full-time — making quilts is as exciting and rewarding as it was when I first began all those years ago.

CRAZY QUILTS

When we think of Victorian crazy quilts, we think of their rich colours and textures, their exotic fabrics and the extensive use of hand-embroidered stitches and embroidered representational motifs reminiscent of a past era. My first crazy quilts were greatly influenced by photographs of these Victorian quilts and I still love them. The time comes, however, when one must move on. The quilts in this chapter show the directions I have taken.

COLOURS OF THE DAY

'Colours of the Day' uses colour to evoke emotion and mood and the changes in attitudes and feelings experienced during the day. The embellishments represent the experiences and activities, the routines and discoveries, the order and disorder of the day. The prospect of making another quilt, using the techniques of 'Colours of the Day', provided a challenge to move on and explore a more abstract adaptation of crazy patchwork.

This quilt was inspired by a June day in Canberra. Winter in Canberra is cold. It is often bleak and sometimes wet and windy. It can also be still and golden. There is a feeling of heaviness and confinement. Suddenly and without warning the sun bursts through and there are wonderful splashes of golden light, like strokes from a paint brush, on water, grass, trees and roofs. The day comes alive. I've called this quilt 'Fog Rising'.

The use of small blocks, placed in a rotated position, provides a greater opportunity to create detail and interest. Fabrics with a rich sheen have been used to provide light, energy and movement; dull, textured fabrics with subdued tones have been used to imply the monochromatic foggy scene. I have also used net to give a sense of depth and of 'seeing into' the fog.

This workshop seeks to explore concepts of colour, line and texture as they coalesce in the crazy patchwork style. This is not a complete process because, while it involves learning techniques such as those of balancing colour and texture, of applied piecing and of embroidery stitches (with particular emphasis on variation and combination of stitches), it is much more the signposting of a long and rewarding journey which the participant must take on her or his own.

Each crazy quilt is unique, because of the random shapes, the individuality of the fabrics and the hand-embroidery. It is not really feasible to provide a design or drawing for such a quilt. No two blocks are the same and the quilt evolves as each one is completed. Rather, I have sought to provide techniques with the intention of offering a methodology which can be used to create a similar quilt.

FABRICS AND NOTIONS

The choice of fabric is highly individual, so a precise specification of fabrics for this quilt is not possible. The following suggestions, some practical, some conceptual, should serve. For the foundation, you will need any cotton or cotton-blend fabric which has a firm and even weave. You will also need:

■ a variety of metallic fabrics and fabrics which have a rich sheen, for the sun areas;

■ a variety of fabrics with a dull lustre for the fog areas;

■ blue net;

■ a selection of metallic embroidery threads, cotton embroidery threads, wool threads, beads and laces to embellish the quilt; and

■ fabric, such as homespun, for the backing.

PIECING

From the foundation fabric, cut out a number of 3 1/8 in (8 cm) squares. You will need approximately 150 for this quilt. This measurement includes a seam allowance of 1/4 in (6 mm). For ease of use, place the cut squares on a pin.

RANDOM STRIP PIECING

Beginning in the middle of the quilt with the 'light' areas, pin the first light strip to the foundation block (Fig. 1). Align the next strip on the first one, with the right side down, and stitch it in place (Fig. 2).

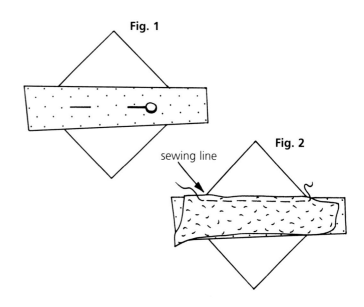

Fig. 1

Fig. 2

sewing line

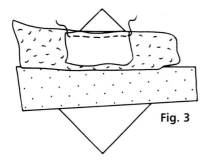

Fig. 3

Fold it out and press it flat, so the next strip can be pinned in place (Fig. 3). Continue applying pieces of fabric in this way until the top half of the foundation has been covered, then rotate the block and cover the bottom in the same way.

RANDOM LOG CABIN PIECING

Random strip piecing is used in the areas where an impression of open space and distance is needed. Where a dense pattern, implying foliage, say, is required, random Log Cabin technique, as shown in figures 4–7, is recommended. Begin with a random shape in the centre and apply the strips in a clockwise direction. An important note – always press each seam before applying the next piece of fabric.

Where a change of fabric is required within a strip, join the pieces together before applying them to the block.

As each block is covered with the applied fabric, press and trim the edges and threads, then arrange the completed blocks on a pin board (Fig. 8).

As the quilt begins to grow, you will need to adjust your choice of fabrics to accord with your preconceived concept. The stillness of the newly exposed sky in 'Fog Rising' is enhanced by using one fabric, opening up the space. The wooded foreground uses dark, rather cold fabrics, with a suggestion of warmth coming from their lustre and sheen.

When the quilt has reached its desired end, join the blocks in strips, beginning with the diagonal strip running from the top left-hand corner to the bottom right-hand corner. Join all the strips in this way. Press all the seams open, then pin the strips to the board for a final check.

Assemble the quilt by joining the strips together, matching the seam lines. Press, then carefully trim, the excess triangles on each side of the quilt (Fig. 9).

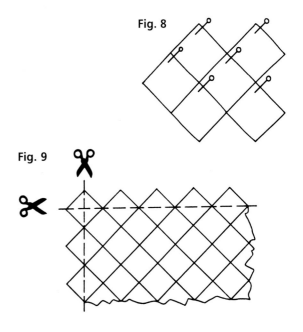

Fig. 8

Fig. 9

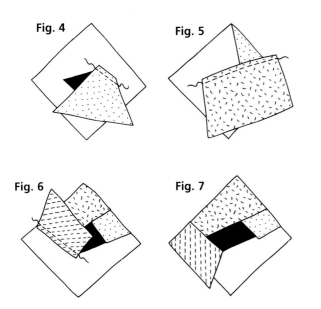

Fig. 4

Fig. 5

Fig. 6

Fig. 7

EMBELLISHING

Baste in place any laces or other embellishments. In 'Fog Rising' I used these laces to suggest the trunks of pine trees. Also, baste in place any additional strips of metallic or shiny fabric, where the sun is making its way into the fog. Arrange the layers of blue net over the fog areas.

French knots Using a variegated woollen yarn, I added French knots to provide additional texture. They can represent rocks or pebbles, or buds on a bush. Complementary beads add light to the area.

Laced running stitch This stitch, worked with embroidery thread, has been used to hold the net in place. Use a single strand for the running stitch and a double strand for the lacing. I find it easier to reverse the needle and use the eye to lace through the running stitches.

Straight stitch This is a useful stitch to hold uneven edges in place.

BORDER

Surround the finished work with a border of plain fabric – black works well with crazy patchwork. The width is a matter of individual judgment, but it needs to balance the overall design well.

ASSEMBLING

Cut the backing fabric the same size as the quilt top. With the right sides together, carefully pin and sew around the edge, leaving an 8 in (20 cm) opening at the bottom.

Trim the triangles off the corners, then gently pull the quilt through the opening, easing the corners into right angles. Press the quilt carefully, then close the opening, using a slipstitch.

TYING

Hold the layers together with a tied stitch, which is repeated in the apex of each block to prevent sagging. Pin both layers together at the apex of each block on the top of the quilt. Turn the quilt over and work from the back. Use two strands of embroidery thread in colours corresponding with the front of the quilt to tie the layers together, using a reef knot. After knotting, cut the threads, leaving 3/4 in (2 cm) tails. Remove the pins as each tie is secured.

EMBROIDERY

Feather stitch The most popular and effective embroidery stitch in crazy patchwork is the feather stitch. Its variations are numerous and quick to execute. It can create the illusion of foliage and is a strong stitch, which is ideal for holding appliquéd pieces in place. I have worked feather stitch in a silver thread to hold the lace pieces in place on this quilt.

The pine tree foliage is also created by feather stitches in three different shades of green embroidery thread. Using a single strand for this work provides more opportunity for detail.

Feather stitch in gold and variegated metallic threads has also been used to extend the beads of light across the light areas. The larger the stitch, the greater the light it will hold.

FOG RISING
$41^{1}/_{2}$ in x $36^{1}/_{2}$ in (105 cm x 93 cm)

BARRIER REEF SAMPLER
48 in x 50 in (122 cm x 127 cm)

IMAGES OF THE BARRIER REEF

EILEEN CAMPBELL

Since beginning quiltmaking in 1983, I have become more and more interested in appliqué. Flora and fauna, whether real or imagined, are what I enjoy working with most. My appliqué designs seem to have evolved along pictorial lines, although I still get much pleasure from creating geometric and traditional designs. To be honest, I do not know where my work is going. I just know that appliqué is my love and that there is still a lot to discover and explore. So, in each project that I do, I try to incorporate something I have not tried before, whether it be painting, embroidery, larger three-dimensional appliqués, or whatever seems appropriate.

I think Australian quiltmaking is very exciting. As a group we have taken traditional quiltmaking and given it a uniquely Australian flavour. Australians are not afraid to use colour, clear colours, colours that sing. Together with colour, the designs in general have a certain boldness and freedom. These things I feel are our greatest assets.

This sampler quilt uses appliqué with three-dimensional techniques and free-machine embroidery. The appliqué pieces range from the traditional single piece of fabric applied directly to the background to padded pieces, made separately then padded again as they are applied.

For a soft lacy effect, some of the machine-embroidery is first stitched onto a foundation which is later 'ironed away'. Other machine-embroidery is worked directly on the background. The combination of all these techniques opens up a wide range of possibilities for three-dimensional work.

Detail of 'Barrier Reef Sampler'

The panel sizes, patterns and instructions for the techniques are given. You could use these as a basis for your own quilt design. The same elements have been used in the large quilt 'Marnie's Seagulls Visit the Reef', which is an extension of the sampler.

PLANNING THE DESIGN

WHERE DO YOU BEGIN?

Collect pictures, photographs and ideas to fit with your chosen topic, then rough out your designs. Each appliqué piece will need to be drawn exactly, but be prepared to change your mind as you go. What looks good on paper is not necessarily the best when translated into fabric.

If you are using a lot of appliqué in a project, give some thought to the size of the pieces you will have to manoeuvre under the machine. You can, of course, keep the whole project to a small or medium size or, alternatively, work in panels. In this way, you could have the same scene running across all the panels, or seasonal scenes, morning-noon-and-night and so on or, as in this quilt, create scenes on a common theme that are not continuous, for example, tropical flowers, mangrove vegetation, and reef fish. The panels can then have either fixed borders or loosely defined borders, with the scenes spilling from one panel to another. Either way, it makes some of the

appliqué easier to manage. Deciding on the panel size will also determine to some extent the size of the motifs. It doesn't matter whether the items are to scale, as long as the overall design is balanced. Work on each panel separately, putting any overlapping motifs in place at the last possible moment.

Borders, except for corners, can be appliquéd before being attached.

FABRIC AND EMBELLISHMENTS

Collect fabrics which will provide a variety of textures. Almost any fabric can be used with the fusible webbing technique, although some fabrics will need protection from the direct heat of the iron.

Beads and rhinestones add an extra quality. Flatbacked rhinestones can be attached with gemstone glue and give a wonderful sparkle and life to eyes. Beads can also be used as eyes, to emphasise flower centres or to highlight areas.

THE APPLIQUE METHOD

For fixing the appliqué, I use double-sided fusible webbing with tracing paper on one side. This makes appliqué very simple, provided you remember one thing – your design must be drawn in reverse on the fusible webbing.

Detail of 'Barrier Reef Sampler'

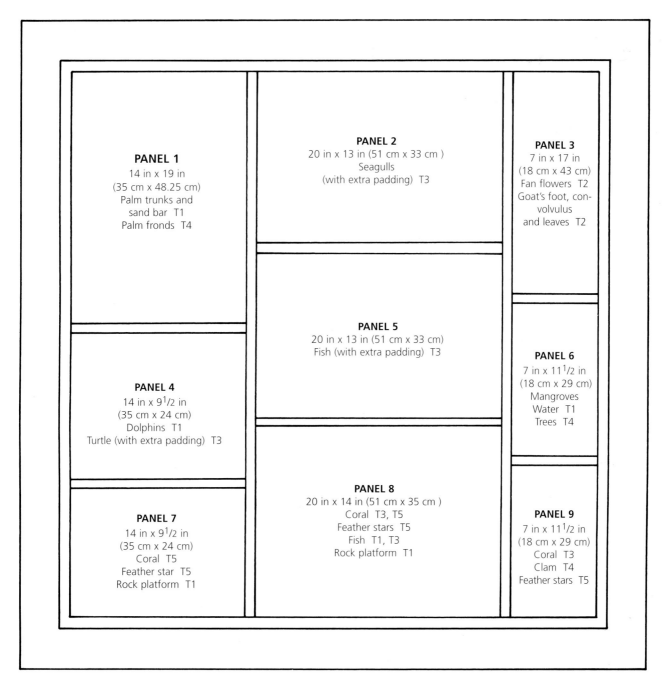

PANEL 1
14 in x 19 in
(35 cm x 48.25 cm)
Palm trunks and
sand bar T1
Palm fronds T4

PANEL 2
20 in x 13 in (51 cm x 33 cm)
Seagulls
(with extra padding) T3

PANEL 3
7 in x 17 in
(18 cm x 43 cm)
Fan flowers T2
Goat's foot, con-
volvulus
and leaves T2

PANEL 5
20 in x 13 in (51 cm x 33 cm)
Fish (with extra padding) T3

PANEL 4
14 in x 9^1/$_2$ in
(35 cm x 24 cm)
Dolphins T1
Turtle (with extra padding) T3

PANEL 6
7 in x 11^1/$_2$ in
(18 cm x 29 cm)
Mangroves
Water T1
Trees T4

PANEL 8
20 in x 14 in (51 cm x 35 cm)
Coral T3, T5
Feather stars T5
Fish T1, T3
Rock platform T1

PANEL 7
14 in x 9^1/$_2$ in
(35 cm x 24 cm)
Coral T5
Feather star T5
Rock platform T1

PANEL 9
7 in x 11^1/$_2$ in
(18 cm x 29 cm)
Coral T3
Clam T4
Feather stars T5

Sashing is ^{3}/$_4$ in (2 cm) wide
Borders are 3 in (7.5 cm) wide
Quilt is 50 in x 49 in (130 cm x 128 cm)
before quilting

TECHNIQUES
T1   Basic fusible-webbing method
T2   Free-form unpadded
T3   Free-form padded
T4   Free-machine embroidery
T5   Free-machine embroidery on heat-
     dissolving stabiliser

On the following pages, there are a few Barrier Reef motifs to start you off. They are no particular size; enlarge or reduce them on a photocopier.

First, you must reverse the image that you will put on the webbing. To do this, hold or tape your design onto a light box or to a window with the daylight shining through it. Trace over the design lines. The back of the paper now has your design in reverse marked on it.

Draw each part of a motif that will be on a different fabric separately. Where one piece adjoins another, allow a bare 1/4 in (6 mm) margin on the piece that will lie beneath the front piece.

Trace the reversed image onto the paper side of the webbing. Cut out the traced motif, leaving a bare 1/4 in (6 mm) margin all around. If you have many pieces to be cut from the same fabric, you can trace them in a block and handle them as one at this stage.

Using a medium-heat, dry iron, press the rough side of the webbing onto the back of the appliqué fabric. Cut out the traced shapes exactly.

When you have cut out the appliqués, decide where you will place them on the background fabric, then peel the backing paper from the webbing on each of the appliqués. Making sure that all the underlaps are in place, and using a medium-heat dry iron, press the pieces into position.

Back your work with an iron-on stabiliser extending 1 in (2.5 cm) beyond all the appliqué pieces. You might use an iron-on tear-away stabiliser where the backing is to be removed, or iron-on stabiliser where it is to stay in place. Stitch the pieces in place. The stabiliser may be torn away afterwards.

THREE-DIMENSIONAL APPLIQUE
Free-form unpadded appliqués This is the particular technique used for the tropical flowers and leaves in Panel 3.

Follow the steps for the appliqué method up to the cutting out of the pieces. Cut a piece of backing fabric large enough to hold all the appliqués (flowers, leaves, etc) plus 3/8 in (1 cm) all around. If the backs of your finished appliqués are likely to show, then choose an appropriate fabric for the backs.

Depending on how firm you want the appliqués,

MARNIE'S SEAGULLS VISIT THE REEF
73 1/2 in x 83 1/2 in (222 cm x 186 cm)

cut either one or two pieces of iron-on stabiliser the same size as the backing fabric. Fuse one or two layers of the stabiliser to the back of the backing fabric.

Peel the tracing paper from the fusible webbing on the appliqués and arrange them on top of the stabiliser. Fuse them into place. Satin stitch around the edges of the appliqués.

Some machine- or hand-embroidery can be done at this stage – for example, stamens on flowers or veins on leaves. You might want to use further embroidery to attach the appliqués to your project.

Cut out the appliqués. It is easiest to use a small pair of sharp scissors and angle them underneath your work as you cut, being very careful not to cut the satin stitch threads. If you do cut a thread (as always happens), use a fray stopper or a drop of clear craft glue on the end of a toothpick to prevent the stitching from unravelling.

If the cut edges of the stabiliser are too visible, colour them carefully with a fabric marker pen.

Free-form padded appliqués   This technique was used for the tropical fish, seagulls and coral in Panel 8.

Prepare the pieces as for the three-dimensional appliqué, but using only one layer of iron-on stabiliser. Cut a piece of iron-on Pellon interfacing the same size as the backing fabric. If this is not available, use ordinary Pellon and fusible webbing.

Cut a piece of fusible webbing the same size as the Pellon and fuse them together. Carefully peel the tracing paper from the webbing and you now have Pellon which you can fuse to the backing. Use baking parchment between the Pellon and the iron.

Peel the tracing paper from the appliqué pieces and fuse them to the backing, again using baking parchment underneath the iron. Satin stitch, embellish, cut out and finish the pieces in the same way as for the unpadded appliqué.

ATTACHING THE PIECES

In this project, the many padded appliqué pieces were attached to the main background both before and after it was quilted.

Coral can be attached at its base into a seam or with monofilament thread within a panel. Using free-machining, catch the coral at various points, so that the pieces will not droop, but in such a way that they still look free and give a three-dimensional appearance. Some branches of coral, especially near the bottom of a piece, can be given a quilted outline in monofilament thread as they are attached, to accentuate them more.

Birds and fish can be attached with monofilament thread, free-machining very close to the satin stitching around the body. Leave the fins free for fish. Birds' wings can be angled slightly against the back-

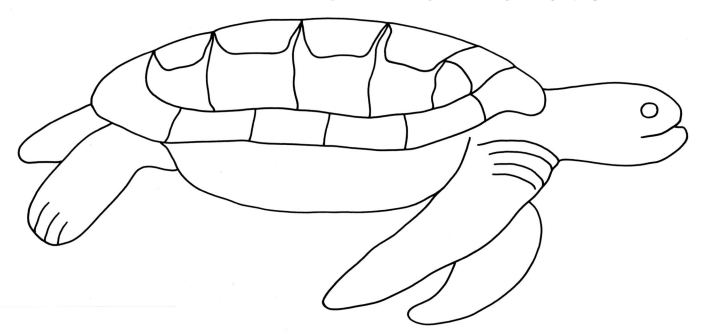

ground fabric and caught at the tips and along one edge. As well as the padding that the Pellon provides, the bodies of birds or fish can be further padded as they are attached. To do this, stitch halfway around your creature's body and, using a small amount of polyester filling, stuff the body before completing the stitching. A satay stick, or something similar, is very useful for hard-to-reach corners and for evening out the filling.

THREADS

Best results are achieved using machine-embroidery rayon thread, especially for the satin stitching. Number 40 thread is good. Polycotton threads can also be used, but they will generally look more chunky and do not give the same sheen.

For a heavier look, a number 30 rayon embroidery thread can be used or, for some free-machining which needs to stand out more, try Cotona 30.

There is a wide range of shiny metallic threads available. The easiest to use are the smooth-finish ones. These are excellent for highlights and for special effects.

Thicker threads which will not go through the machine, as used in outlining on the panels, can be couched down. Use a braiding foot and zigzag stitch: less than 1/16 in long by less than 1/16 in wide (about 1.5 mm wide by 1.5 mm long) is a good average.

In the bobbin, use Bobbinfil or a fine polycotton when appliquéing directly onto your background. If you are stitching the three-dimensional appliqués, it is best to use the same thread for the top and for the bobbin, as the colour will then be even on all the visible edges.

For all appliqué and machine-embroidery, it is best to use a Metalfil or System N needle, size 75 or 80. This needle has a bigger eye and helps to keep the thread from breaking.

STITCHING

Satin stitching For satin stitching, loosen the top tension by at least one stop. Your aim is to have the satin stitching pull underneath slightly, so that the top thread is seen on either side of the bobbin thread. For most appliqués, the satin stitch width is up to

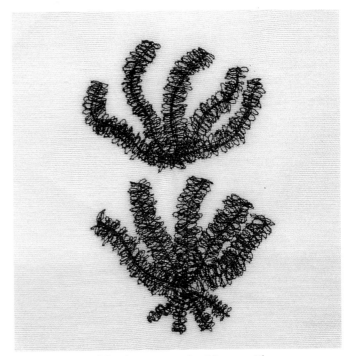

Two sections of feather star embroidery on Thermogaze

1/16 in (between 1.5 and 2 mm). Your stitches should rest mostly on the appliqué piece, coming over only slightly onto the background. Set the stitch length so that the stitching appears to be a solid line, but not so close that the stitches bunch up. The complex mixtures of fabrics used can affect your machine settings, so practise sewing on some samples of the fused layers and stabilisers used in each particular project.

Begin and end the stitching with a few fastening stitches on one spot, or pull the top thread through and tie off at the back.

Complete all satin stitch before cutting out

The aim is to always sew at right angles to the edge of the appliqué piece you are stitching. Where you need to change the angle to go around a curve, stop with the needle in the wide part of the curve, lift the presser foot, turn your work slightly and do a few more stitches. Repeat this pivoting step as many times as you find it necessary to complete stitching the curve smoothly.

For points on the ends of leaves and so on, it is not necessary to taper the stitch. Continue to the top of the point. Leave the needle down and turn your work. Raise the needle and reposition the work, so that your first stitching in the other direction covers the previous couple of stitches. This will give you a blunt point and is very easy to do without affecting the good appearance.

Free-machine embroidery To do this, you will need a darning foot and also be able to lower the feed dogs or cover them with a plate.

Set your machine for straight stitching with a stitch width and length set at 0. Tension should be normal, although you may have to lower it a little, depending on your stitching. Bring the bobbin thread up to the top of your work and hold both threads as you take the first few stitches. After that you can stitch in any direction. Some appliqués are best stitched using this technique – for example, the palm trees in Panel 1 and the mangrove trees in Panel 6. Attach the appliqué pieces using the fusible webbing technique, but instead of satin stitching,

hold the pieces down with free-machine stitching. You might use a combination of stitches: satin stitch for the trunk and free-machining for the leaves. Free-machining is also used to embellish appliqués, defining the veins in leaves, the fish fins and so on.

Free-machining using a heat-dissolving stabiliser, such as Thermogaze This technique was used for some corals and feather stars, some of which are made in two pieces, then joined (see page 41). Thermogaze is a heat-vanishing muslin which you can put into a hoop and embroider on. Ironing will turn Thermogaze into a brown powder that can be brushed away. Thermogaze must be stored in a dark place.

When embroidering on the Thermogaze, use the same thread on the top and in the bobbin. Make sure that all your embroidery lines are connected so that your piece will not fall apart, when the supporting Thermogaze is removed. You can draw on it easily with a pencil if you need guidelines.

Put the embroidered Thermogaze between two sheets of baking parchment when you press it.

To attach this piece, before or after quilting, use the same coloured thread or a clear monofilament thread. Free machine it in place, leaving some areas unattached for a three-dimensional effect.

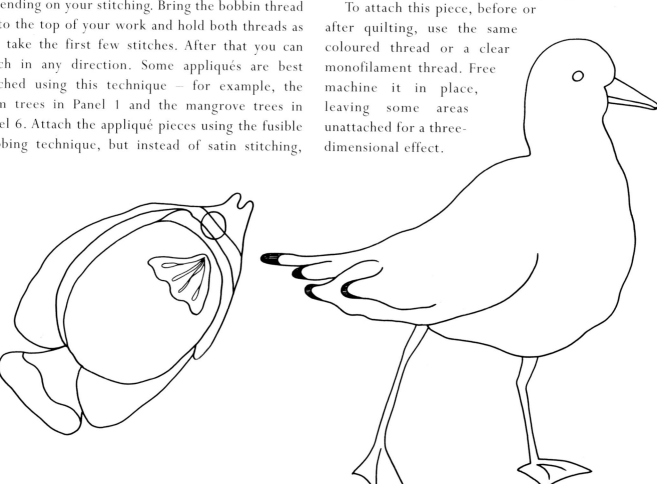

TALL POPPIES
12¹/₄ in x 17¹/₄ in (31 cm x 43.5 cm)

FABULOUS FLOWERS

CYNTHIA MORGAN

Through my quilts, I seek to make the viewer more aware of the beauty of natural environment which is gradually being eroded by man's uncontrolled intrusion. The very techniques used, the interplay of light and movement, and the tactile appeal of the quilt speak directly to the senses.

My three very different quilts which illustrate this workshop were created using diverse techniques. I will describe how to create a rich background, as well as the embellishments which make each quilt unique. I hope you will be encouraged to make your own fabulous flower quilts.

DESIGN

Begin with a picture or photograph of a flower, or part of it, and enlarge it on a colour photocopier to use as an inspiration. The photocopy also acts as a guide to colour and scale, but it is only a jumping-off point from which the final design will eventually evolve. The artist's work is not an exact replica or a copy of the photocopy, but an impression of a personal perception. Indeed, the work resulting from this formal beginning can be abstracted into pure fantasy flowers.

PAINTING THE DESIGN

All the fabrics must be washed in hot water and soap powder to remove any chemical sizing. The backgrounds for these three quilts are all cotton, dyed with cold-water, fibre-reactive dyes, such as Procion MX and Drimarine K, which were developed for use on natural fibres.

'Fabulous Flowers' was dyed using the polychromatic dyeing process which results in a detailed realistic image without the use of a resist, using a silk-screen process. The dye is first painted directly onto the screen, then transferred to the fabric with a mixture of sodium alginate and soda as the screen printing medium. Use a screen stretched with a fine polyester silk mesh because fibre-reactive dyes have no affinity with polyester, so the design sits on top of the synthetic fibres until it is released by the screen-printing process. Dye powders, mixed with water only, are painted, as for watercolour painting, directly on the back of the screen which will be in contact with the fabric. As the image is reversed when it is printed, paint the design in reverse on the screen. To make this easier, draw the design lightly on the other (inside) surface of the screen.

The amount of water used to dilute the dye determines the strength of the colour. Test the colour first on a piece of spare fabric, remembering that the colour will be paler when it is dry. The dyes must be completely dissolved to prevent any undissolved powder from clogging the screen mesh and not printing, leaving a white spot. As the dye dries lighter than when it is freshly applied, and there is a slight loss of dye in the final washing, paint the design slightly darker than desired for the final result.

Begin by painting the darker toned areas, then any spots of dye on the lighter areas can be cleaned off with a dampened cotton ball before the area is painted. In this quilt, 'Fabulous Flowers', the background and leaves were painted first.

If colours are applied wet-on-wet, they will run or merge into one another creating a third colour. To avoid this, and where a distinct edge is required, dry the area first with a hair dryer, before applying dye to the adjacent section. To change any part of the design, simply wipe it out with a damp cotton ball, tissue or scrap of fabric, then allow the screen to dry completely, before this area is repainted.

Backgrounds should be painted in one session. If, for any reason, part of an area dries out, avoid the appearance of a harsh line by painting a pale wash of the colour used over the dry area, then continue with the painting. As the parts of the screen dry, the colours will appear dull when compared with the wet dye being applied. Tilt the screen and view it at an angle to see the true depth of colour. When the painting is completed, leave it to dry before attempting to print.

PRINTING

Make up the printing medium, following the recipe on page 49, and leave it to stand overnight. Prepare the printing bed with an old blanket, topped with an old sheet. Tape them flat to a table and make sure there are no wrinkles. Stretch the prewashed and ironed fabric to be printed over this surface with its edges held down by masking tape so they don't lift when the screen is removed.

Place the screen face down with the painted surface touching the fabric and the sides of the screen parallel to the straight grain of the fabric. Place the squeegee at the end of the paper well at one end of the screen and pour the printing medium into the well. Pass the squeegee several times up and down the screen to release the dye for one print.

After printing, remove the screen and the

FABULOUS FLOWERS
29 in x 36¹/4 in (73 cm x 92 cm)

squeegee and wash them in a trough or under the garden hose. It is important to do this properly so the printing medium does not dry on the screen and clog the mesh.

Leave the printed fabric covered with plastic for twenty-four hours or more to allow the dye to cure. The urea in the mixture keeps the fabric damp and aids the curing process. After curing, rinse the fabric in warm water to remove the printing medium, then wash it in hot water, using mild soap flakes, such as Lux, or a pure detergent, such as Lysapol or Synthrapol. Adding 1 teaspoon (5 g) of soda ash per 1³/4 pints (1 litre) of water will assist the fixation of the dyes. Dry the fabric in the shade.

The borders and bindings of 'Fabulous Flowers'

were dyed in the same way on a separate screen.

I photographed the extraordinary 'Wreath Lechenaultia' (page 48) flowers in a cemetery in Western Australia, where, looking like wreaths tossed about by the wind, they grew wild in the dry, powdered rock soil.

For 'Tall Poppies' (page 44), I wanted an out-of-focus background of greenery with hints of colour. Part of this would be seen between the mosaic pieces and some would be seen as 'negative space' at the top of the panel.

The backgrounds of both 'Wreath Lechenaultia' and 'Tall Poppies' were created by painting directly onto dampened fabric which had been sprayed with a mixture of soda and water (see page 49). The damp-

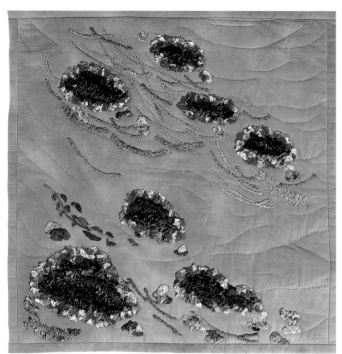

WREATH LECHENAULTIA
24 in (60 cm) square

ness allows the dyes to spread easily. Mix the dye powder with chemical water, minus the soda (see page 49) by adding the dye powder on top of the water. The dye can be brushed, rolled or poured on, depending on the effect that is required. After the painting is completed, the dyed fabric is left to cure overnight, then washed in warm, soapy water to remove any chemicals. The dye is now fast and the fabric ready to be embellished.

EMBELLISHMENT

Although 'Fabulous Flowers' required very little additional embellishment – which was added after the top was machine-quilted – this embellishment has tremendous impact. It adds an essential illusory third dimension to the quilt.

Silk satin and cotton were hand-dyed with the same colours as the flowers on the quilt top. They were then fused together with a fusible webbing, before being cut to the shape of buds, and the three-petalled centres of some of the flowers. These petals were embellished with machine-embroidery before being attached. Fused cotton fabrics, stitched to simulate veins, made the three-dimensional leaves which were strategically placed.

Borders and bindings for the quilt were attached in the usual way.

'Tall Poppies' has an out-of-focus mosaic background, made up of tiny pieces of dyed fabrics. I lined the green background with tear-away stabiliser and pinned it to the design board. I then cut individual pieces of fabric and pinned them to the background to create the impression of greenery and flowers. Each piece was then adhered to the background with a small dab of non-acidic glue and left to dry. Finally, these pieces were sewn to the background, using fine monofilament thread.

To decide on the placement of the major flowers, I cut petals from yellow paper. To hand-dye the polyester fabrics for the flowers, they were first painted with a polysol disperse dye solution, then allowed to dry before being heat-set using an iron with no steam holes. To do this, place the fabric between two sheets of brown paper and iron with pressure for less than a minute. When the fabric cools, cut petal shapes slightly larger than the finished size. To prevent fraying, seal the edges by stroking them with a hot soldering iron.

Where silk was to be used for the petals, the silk was first fused to a backing of the dyed polyester and the edges sealed in the same way.

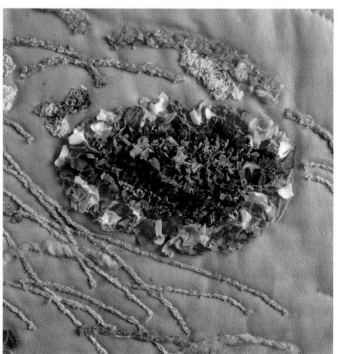

Detail of 'Wreath Lechenaultia'

Detail of 'Fabulous Flowers'

This use of polyester allowed for free-standing petals which were hand-sewn in place with invisible thread, adding the third dimension to the quilt.

In 'Wreath Lechenaultia' the flowers surround the grass-like foliage which was emulated by stiffening various hand-dyed green strips with fabric stiffener, then cutting each strip in parallel lines with $^1/_4$ in (5 mm) of the strip left uncut. This uncut section was machine-sewn down the centre in the middle of each wreath, using several strips to mix the greens in each clump. For the individual florets, I folded small pieces of different pink silks and cotton fabrics and hand-sewed them at the point of the fold. The exposed edges were painted with a fray stopper. Massed, unravelled threads were hand-sewn to depict the yellow flowers growing nearby. Polyester leaves and sticks made from couched hand-dyed yarns and chenille completed the scene. Finally, I hand-quilted the negative spaces.

RECIPES

TO PRE-SODA FABRIC

Mix $^1/_2$ cup of washing soda in $1^3/_4$ pt (1 litre) of hot water. Pour it into a spray bottle and spray it evenly over the fabric until it is all damp. Do not pre-soda silk.

CHEMICAL WATER

Mix 1 teaspoon of resist salt, 1 teaspoon of Calgon and 10 tablespoons of urea in 2 cups of hot water to dissolve. Add 2 cups of cold water. The mixture will keep indefinitely in the refrigerator or for two or three months at room temperature. Immediately before using, add 1 teaspoon of bicarbonate of soda and a $^1/_2$ teaspoon of washing soda per cup of chemical water.

PRINTING MEDIUM

Dissolve $6^1/_2$ oz (200 g) of urea in approximately 16 fl oz (500 ml) of hot water and allow to cool. When it is cold, add more cold water to make it up to 30 fl oz (850 ml). Sprinkle $1^3/_4$ oz (50 g) of sodium alginate, or the appropriate product and amount for silk, into the water and stir or beat continuously. Never add water to dry sodium alginate. Leave the mix for five or ten minutes, then refrigerate. The mixture will keep indefinitely in the refrigerator.

Before using, dissolve $^1/_2$ oz (15 g) of soda ash and $^1/_2$ oz (15 g) of resist salt in a little hot water, then add it to the sodium-alginate solution, which should then be about $1^3/_4$ pt (1 litre) with the consistency of runny honey. If more water is needed, add more soda. If only a portion of the sodium-alginate solution is required, add soda ash and resist salt in the same proportions.

KEY #1
38¹/4 in x 59 in (97 cm x 150 cm)

CREATIVE QUILT DESIGN

CHRISTA SANDERS

Everybody has the ability to be creative, but our creativity shows up in different areas. This is a kind of natural selection which benefits the whole. There is no need to strive for absolute perfection, but we do have a responsibility to identify and nurture our talents. Much has been said about the importance of a healthy lifestyle – I believe creativity is an important part of a healthy life.

No rigid set of rules helps us to be creative – a more gentle approach is required. Translating experiences into a visual form may seem to some people to be impossible and may cause them to give up. To move forward in any field involves the risk of disapproval and criticism. What is needed to overcome these fears is a spirit of adventure and faith in one's own strengths. The road to success is littered with mistakes and failures, and an acceptance of this takes away some of the hurt.

Designing an original quilt demands courage, a willingness to venture into unknown territory and take responsibility. We have to become independent.

Embarking on a creative project, it is necessary to have a plan which brings together all the components, such as the symbols, colour, line, texture and skills involved in the execution. This plan is called the design.

DESIGN

To some, an original quilt design seems an impossible goal. Design is all around us – in our houses, schools, churches and cities, as well as in our daily lives. In this sense we are all designers. Therefore, a

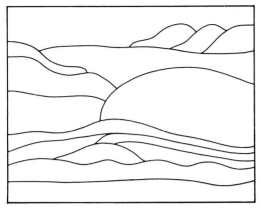

Fig. 1 Outline of 'Key #2'

Fig. 2 Detailed structure of 'Key #2'

creative quilt design begins with the kind of knowledge we have all absorbed and an inner sense of direction. Being in tune with and responding to emotions are vital ingredients for an original design.

Research is also an important factor of design. A quilter approaching a new quilt depicting a particular flower would do well to learn something about that flower. Where does it live? Does it have associations with a special happening, celebration or ceremony?

At the beginning of the creative quilt design, the subject should be clearly developed 'in the head' of the artist with the help of visual materials collected during research.

SYMBOLS

We often speak symbolically in expressions like 'touch wood' or 'an eye for an eye' which come from many sources. The alphabet, numbers, musical notes and the like are also symbolic language. Symbols are all around us and are an important tool of communication; using them in a quilt design can communicate a general sense of the subject.

Symbols need not be ancient and universal. They can be very personal and may not necessarily be immediately obvious to other viewers.

SYMBOLS AND DESIGN OF 'KEY #1' AND 'KEY #2'

I have lost count of how many quilts I have completed, but each quilt, with its faults and successes, became a preparation for the next one – not always in its degree of technical difficulty, but in working through the various concepts. The quilts 'Key #1' and 'Key #2' followed a series of quilts on angels and continued on into a series called 'Place of Understanding' and 'Key of Understanding'. This whole body of work, which is connected, has been going on for two years and is still not completed.

'Key #1' deals with the question of accumulated knowledge. Information is not knowledge and every individual has to own their truth. My children are not prepared, and should not be prepared, to take on all my knowledge of life. They have to find their own knowledge.

We live in a problematic world; once the key to a problem is discovered, there is a better chance of a solution being found. The key becomes the solution and a much sought-after item. In the design, the shape of the key needed to convey this symbolic strength, with the colour of the key, gold, emphasising its value.

The top of the key has two circles representing opposites. They are attached, but the shapes within the circle suggest that they are separate. Like heaven and earth, male and female, war and peace, these opposites are balanced through the top circle and make the shape of the key complete.

The background shapes are layered. The fabrics and patterns – which included snippets of landscapes, fences, spirals, jugs, the environment, and stairs to climb – were carefully chosen as they also take on important meanings. In the shape of the houses, special places are to be found. Some of these places only have windows to look out of, others have hidden doors, some are warm and cosy, others are dark and uninviting. As a whole, the background is a landscape to move through, seemingly uphill all the way. The colours, dominantly blue and yellow-red, are harmonious.

The fabrics used are cotton, polyester, wool and blends with the key overprinted with fabric paints.

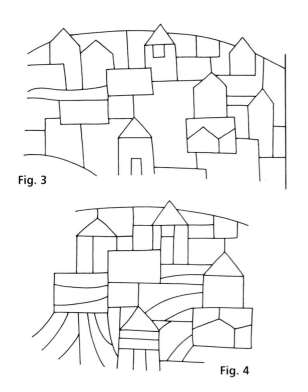

Fig. 3

Fig. 4

LINE

A quilt design obtains its basic effect through line. Firstly, through the initial outline of the quilt design; secondly, through a breaking up of large outline areas into smaller ones; and thirdly, through the quilting line.

Line has great communicative qualities. An image can be gentle, dynamic, relaxed, rugged, strong or poetic, depending on the line. Lines can be straight or curved, and repetition of line makes a pattern.

If a landscape form becomes the quilt design, it is helpful to remember that the whole picture at this stage is more important than the individual shapes. These will take on importance later. To ease the design responsibility, the image can be broken up into sections; for example, cliffs into water and sky, beach into waves and sky, objects into background and foreground (Fig. 1). Above all, a quilt design adds up to careful observation.

Once the outline design is finished, a more detailed structure can be applied (Figs. 2, 3 and 4). Often the quilt demands its own formulation. The details do not have to be decided all at once and areas of uncertainty can be resolved at a later stage.

In 'Key #2', I continued the themes from 'Key #1'. In his book, *Symbolism: A Comprehensive Dictionary* (McFarland and Co. Inc. 1986), Steven Olderr describes three keys. Based on legend and folklore, the key of silver demonstrates psychological understanding, while the key of gold stands for philosophical wisdom. The third, a diamond key, confers the power to act. In this quilt, fragments of a gold and silver key, overprinted on various fabrics, are spread throughout the landscape. This quilt led directly to the next work, 'Key and Place of Understanding'.

COLOUR

Next to design, colour needs careful consideration. Colour theory and the use of the colour wheel gives much direction and provides useful tools; every quilter will benefit from familiarity with some ground rules of how colour behaves.

Never underestimate the impact of colour. Harmony and balance, movement and contrast are achieved by colour choices. Experiments with different combinations, both preferred and familiar as well as those seldom used, will help the designer to come to a final decision.

Colour also evokes mood, so I believe this is reason enough to have a close look at colour in an emotional context.

A combination of colour theory, intuition and knowledge of the colour codes used within our society equip a quilter when considering how to communicate ideas, a meaning or mood. We are greatly influenced by colour through association. Colour means what society says that it means. How difficult it is to imagine a baby girl in blue and a baby boy in pink. If this is not convincing enough, consider the colours of a football team or a national flag.

Knowing how colours work and how they can influence our mood will add another dimension in a quilt design. In my quilts 'Key #1' and 'Key #2' I have used the basic principles of light, medium and dark, both within the large outline shapes and the detailed structure. Contrasts of colour occur, adding to the depth in a design. Painted fabrics increase the colour possibilities.

TEXTURE

Quilts offer a visual and a tactile experience. By combining fabrics which reflect light differently, a richness of imagery can be achieved. How rich is left entirely to the designer. Fabric, commercial or painted, can be the only source, but many quilts today have a variety of surface decorations. Buttons, found objects, embroidery, print, beads, paper, and feathers ... to name but a few. Boundaries can be pushed to suit a quilt design.

CONSTRUCTION

Small sketches and observation will help to formulate your ideas. If you are working with a landscape, break your design into foreground, middle distance and background.

Full-sized cartoons should be drawn up at actual size. I find thin cardboard sheets, joined with tape, adequate for the job.

In my quilt, 'Key #1', the key itself was enlarged from a small drawing to its actual size with the help of a grid. The key and grid are given in figure 5. The background was drawn straight onto the cardboard. In 'Key #2', I worked on small sketches until I was happy with the design, then I transferred the outline design, with the help of a grid, to the full-sized cardboard cartoon. After that, I decided on the details to be present in each section and drew them in.

Each shape becomes a template. There are no short cuts or quick ways to the piecing of these shapes; they all demand individual attention. A consolation is that perhaps this allows for full enjoyment of the colour and fabric choices.

MAKING TEMPLATES

Check your design and make sure you have drawn shapes which you can sew. Join sheets of thin cardboard with tape and transfer your design to them, enlarging it from the sketch to the actual size with the help of a grid. At this point, step back and re-evaluate your design: shapes can be added, simplified or taken out completely.

Trace your design, or sections of it, onto a large sheet of paper for future reference. Mark the grain on the templates and mark the intersection of

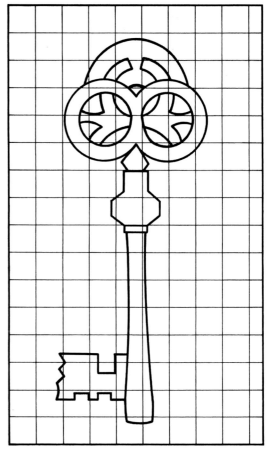

Fig. 5

neighbouring shapes. Then cut out the cardboard pieces. These are your templates.

PIECING

Working on small sections at a time, decide on the colours and fabrics for the number of shapes you feel comfortable with, then cut them out as follows.

Place the right side of the cardboard template on the wrong side of the fabric, and carefully draw around the shape with a sharp pencil or fabric marker pen. Also draw the intersection marks on the wrong side of the fabric.

Do not cut along the pencil/marker pen line as this will be your sewing line. Allow a ¼ in (6 mm) seam allowance when you cut out each piece.

Next, decide on the piecing order. Pin the pieces together, placing the pins very close together on the sewing line. Sew on the pencil line. A back stitch at both ends is optional, but do not stitch across the seams, except where large sections are being joined together. Press the seams to one side.

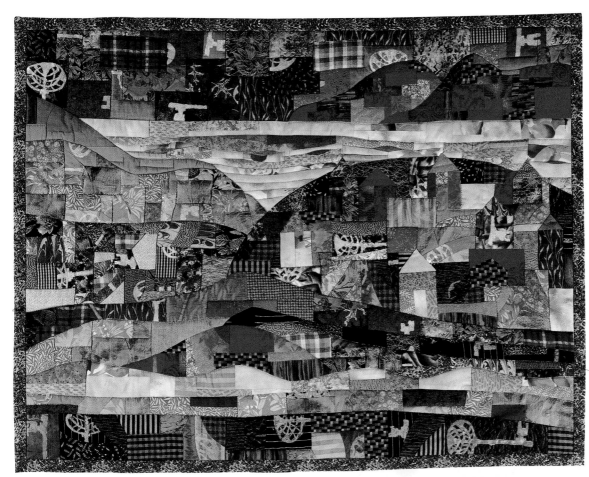

KEY #2
*50 1/2 in x 39 in
(128 cm x 99 cm)*

For curved piecing, place one pin on either side with the concave curved piece on the top and the convex curved piece on the bottom. Continue to pin very closely. If the curves are very tight, clip the fabric in two, three or more places in the concave seam allowance and stitch slowly, easing the needle around the folds of the concave line.

QUILTING

After basting or pinning the three layers to construct the quilt, it's time to consider the quilting. The quilting line can add a whole new dimension to your work. It can be made very visible and enhance other lines throughout the design. It can dominate the whole quilt or be made almost invisible by putting the stitches close to the seams. Intensive surface work can highlight areas.

Many textile artists use their knowledge from related fields like embroidery, weaving or painting and incorporate them into their quilt designs.

A quilt might not bring a football ground full of

Detail of 'Key #2'

people to their feet, but it might make a difference to one person or to several people who identify with the work and read it in their own way, taking from it whatever they need: comfort, celebration, recognition or confrontation.

WAIT FOR ME
27 in x 36¹/4 in (69 cm x 92 cm)

SHADOW WORK AND TRANSPARENT OVERLAY

TRUDY BILLINGSLEY

My development as a textile artist has been and continues to be a great adventure. I have a passion for drawing, moulding and creating with my hands – the result of my love for all the creative arts.

Although I grew up in a very creative environment, where all around me people made things with their hands, I am self-taught.

As I develop a new work, I surround myself with piles of fabrics, interesting threads and trims which all serve to feed my interest and inspiration. The saying, 'Creativity requires chaos before form emerges', certainly seems to apply to this process.

My creative textile garments are the result of an investment of time and of my desire to design and construct something different. From looking, seeing, developing an idea, working it through from sketchbook to swatches to samples, construction of the garment and its marketing, I am interested in it all – and I enjoy wearing my creative garments.

My work is all about developing a theme. The beauty of the environment and an interest in travel have been a great influence and are a constant source of design inspiration. I believe we are not here on earth for a long time, but we are here for a good time. My work is about enjoying life's great gifts and having fun on the journey.

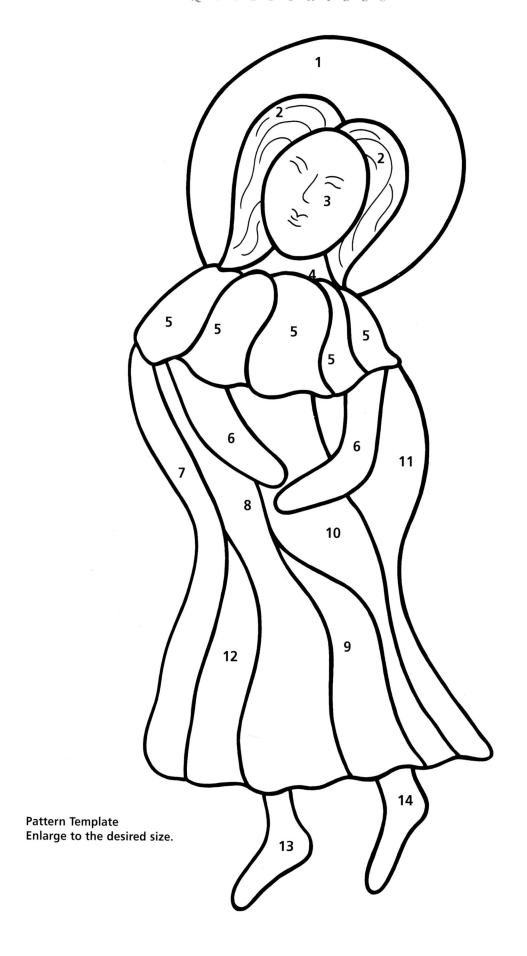

Pattern Template
Enlarge to the desired size.

WHAT IS SHADOW WORK?

Shadow work and transparent overlay are techniques whereby fabrics are trapped between two layers of tulle and secured with stitches. Fine black tulle is preferred because it enhances the colour of the fabric beneath. These prepared areas can then be used to enhance the quilt surface with collage, while still allowing for light and texture.

The effect can be achieved using sheer fabrics: tulle, organza, chiffon, georgette, fine lace, net and so on. When they are trapped between two layers of tulle, a light, delicate image without the hard edges of traditional appliqué is created. Using some or all of the techniques I describe will enable you to include a great variety of objects on the surface of your quilt. Coins, animals, figures, stamps, old documents, drawings, and other memorabilia are all great additions to a quilt. Delicate objects can easily be removed prior to washing. Trees made in this way appear to be more natural with glimpses of sky or landscape visible through the leaves. Reeds and grasses can also be applied using this technique and will give depth to the quilt surface (see detail A).

Shadow-work flowers, made of brightly coloured and overlayed petals with a beaded centre, can be used for collage or to form a sculptured border on a floral quilt or garment (see detail B).

This technique particularly lends itself to representing fish and marine animals, which truly appear to float in their environment (see detail C).

Movement can be achieved with quilting stitches. Hand-dyed and mono-printed lines on sheer fabrics are an excellent way of developing design lines on the surface of a quilt. Petals or leaves can be mono-printed or drawn on with permanent pen, before the top layer of tulle is applied.

Shading and texture can also be achieved by using random shadow work. This is done by placing pieces of transparent fabric on tulle: teased silk and wool tops (silk and wool before they are spun), threads, fabric fragments, cords, braids, lace or manipulated sheer fabrics. Cover with another piece of tulle and secure it with stitches. These textured areas can be used as a background for a scene, such as in the marine scene on the wall cape in detail C.

A memorabilia quilt can be enhanced with delicate old laces applied to the quilt, using this technique. Place the lace between two layers of tulle, before attaching them to the quilt. Fragile pieces, attached to the quilt in this way, can be easily removed before the quilt is washed.

Detail A

MAKE A SHADOW-WORK ANGEL

'Wait for Me' perfectly demonstrates the use of shadow work and transparent overlay. I wanted the angels to appear as though they were passing over and out of the quilt top. The angels were designed and made separately and were then applied to the quilt surface in the plain areas which were specifically designed to accommodate them.

Begin by making a full-scale drawing of the angel, shown opposite. Mark the stitching and the cutting lines (see page 60) and number each piece. Photocopy this drawing – the drawing is the design, the copy will provide the templates.

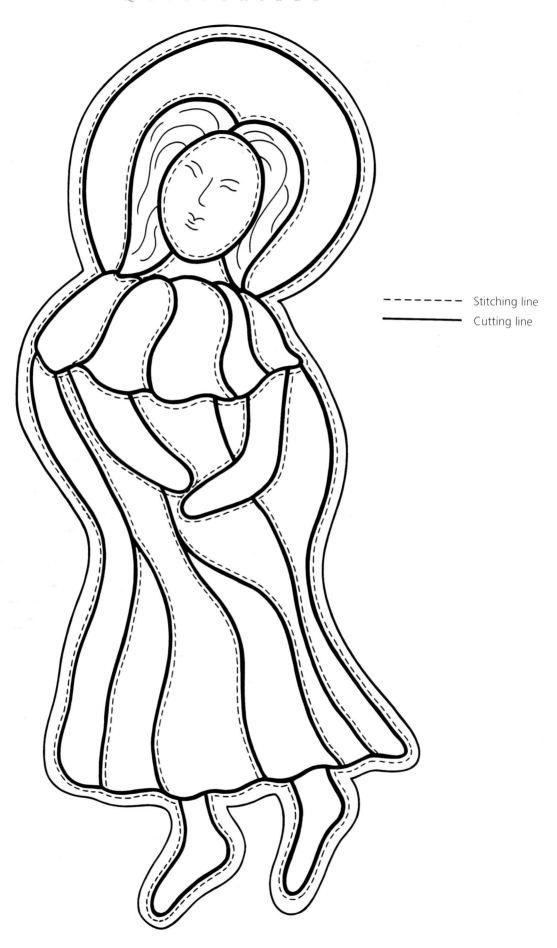

- - - - - - Stitching line
———— Cutting line

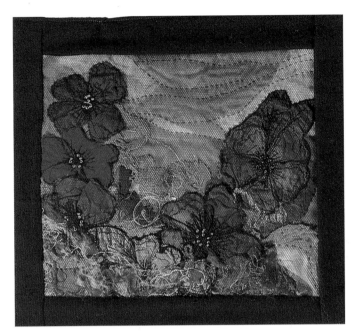

Detail B

quite easy to do with dressmaker's pins.

The angel is now ready to be stitched. This can be done straight onto the quilt or separately and the angel applied later. I placed the angels onto the quilt and stitched them on with a small running stitch using dark thread. Beginning with a back stitch, sew right on the edge of the fabric pieces and through both layers of tulle. Make sure each piece of fabric is secured, then cut away the excess tulle.

The angel's face and the folds of the drapery have been worked in stem stitch and large running stitch, with additional ribbon applied to the drapery. The angel's halo is made from heavy machine-embroidery over a metallic gold fabric. The stars were developed in the stitchery.

Place the design under fine black tulle and secure the corners with pins. Use dressmaker's pins not glass-headed pins, as this type of pin will move through the top layer of tulle.

Cut the pieces from the copy of the design to make the templates. Using the templates, cut out the fabric to the exact size and shape required with no seam allowances, as the pieces are laid edge to edge. Place the cut-out fabrics onto the tulle, following the design drawing, which is underneath. Always place the darker fabrics first, then the lighter ones on top. Secure all the pieces with dressmaker's pins.

Cover the angel with another piece of tulle, making sure it is larger than required for the final design. It can be trimmed to size later. Work all the pins through to catch the top layer of tulle. This is

Detail C

ANY PORT IN A STORM
47¹/4 in x 37¹/2 in (120 cm x 95 cm)

MASTERING THE MADDENING MARINER

ADINA SULLIVAN

The Mariner's Compass block (also known as the Sunburst or Sunflower) is generally thought of as a difficult block to master. It certainly requires patience and precision in drafting and piecing and isn't a block where 'near enough is good enough' applies. It is based, however, on simple geometric rules and, if these rules are followed, the block is quite easy to draft.

Because I consider original design to be the most rewarding facet of quiltmaking, this is a lesson on how to draft the Mariner's Compass to enable you to make your own stunning 'one of a kind' pieces.

I was inspired to attempt the Mariner's Compass block after seeing Judy Mathieson's quilts. I had formulated a method of hand-piecing using freezer paper when working with precision-pieced blocks and striped fabric. The method seemed to suit the madness of the Mariner.

My first Mariner's Compass quilt received a Judges' Commendation in the 1994 Sydney Quilt Festival and, since then, the design has become one of my quilting passions.

I hope this workshop inspires you to share my love of this fascinating block.

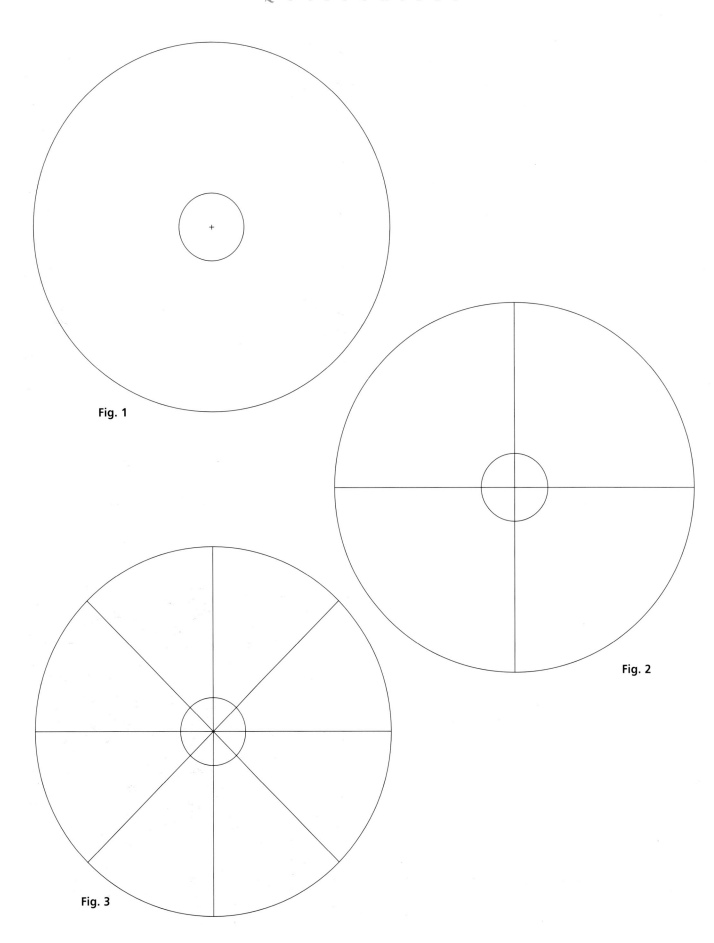

Fig. 1

Fig. 2

Fig. 3

DRAFTING

REQUIREMENTS

2B pencil and sharpener

Eraser

20 in (50 cm) ruler

Fixed compass (with screw mechanism for changing length)

360° protractor

11 in x 17 in (28 cm x 43 cm) paper

Note: A yardstick compass is useful for drawing bigger Mariner's Compasses and a reasonably efficient one can be made by drilling pencil-sized holes in a 20 in (50 cm) wooden ruler and pressing a thumb tack through the opposite end.

Mark the centre of a sheet of 11 in x 17 in (28 cm x 43 cm) paper with a small cross. Set your compass to its maximum width (about 4$7/8$ in (12.5 cm) is average). Place the point of the compass in the centre of the cross and draw a circle. Adjust your compass back to a width of 1$1/2$ in (4 cm). With the point of the compass in the centre of the cross, draw another circle (Fig. 1).

With the centre of the protractor lined up with the cross, mark the points at 0, 90, 180 and 270 degrees on the circle. Connect pairs of opposite points with a light pencil line and extend these lines to touch the outer circle (Fig. 2). These are the primary lines.

Realign the protractor and mark the points at 45, 135, 225 and 315 degrees. Join these marks and extend them as before (Fig. 3). These are the secondary lines.

Draw lines from the points where the primary lines intersect the outer circle to where the secondary lines intersect the inner circle. These are the primary points. Draw lines from the points where the secondary lines intersect the outer circle to where the primary lines intersect the inner circle, stopping the line at the edge of the primary points (Fig. 4). These are the secondary points.

Mark the 22.5 degree points (halfway between the existing points). Lightly join the lines between the circles and use these lines to draw tertiary points in the same way as the primary points were drawn

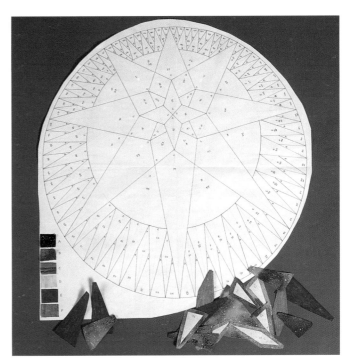

Make a master copy

(Fig. 5). This is a called a sixteen-point Split Mariner's Compass as it is split down the centre.

Remove the lines within the centre circle (Fig. 6) or remove the centre circle (Fig. 7). If you remove the centre (split) lines and the lines within the inner circle, then continue all the point lines to touch the inner circle, it becomes a Sunburst Mariner's Compass (Fig. 8).

Pieces basted to freezer paper

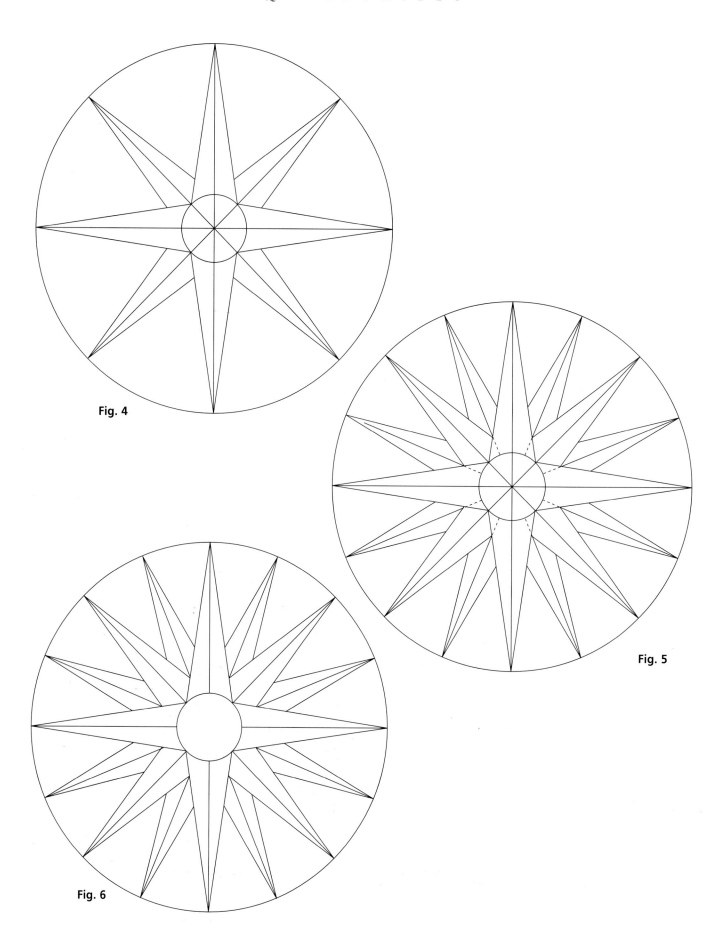

Fig. 4

Fig. 5

Fig. 6

VARIATIONS

The width of the points can be changed by changing the size of the inner circle (a smaller circle gives finer points, a larger circle gives thicker points). Further design changes can be made by ruling lines across the widest part of the points to make another pattern piece (Fig. 9).

Another variation to the basic design is to draft using concentric circles as the bases of the points. These circles may then be used as part of the pattern, straightened or eliminated (Fig. 10).

Concentric circles can also be used to alter the length of the points (Fig. 11).

Mariner's Compass quilts are traditionally made with the number of points divisible by eight (as many as the points of a compass), however it is possible to draft many different variations, simply by dividing the 360° of the protractor to give the required number of points. For example:

- for nine points, mark every 40 degrees;
- for eighteen points, mark every 20 degrees;
- for thirty-six points, mark every 10 degrees;
- for five points, mark every 72 degrees;
- for ten points, mark every 36 degrees;
- for twenty points, mark every 18 degrees; and
- for six points, mark every 60 degrees.

(**Note**: a six-pointed Mariner's Compass will fit into a hexagon and may then be used in an isometric grid.)

It is preferable to use the concentric circle method of drafting to draw these variations. Draft several of these versions until you feel comfortable with them.

EXPANDED PERIMETERS

To make a Mariner's Compass fit into a required shape (as in between the pyramids in my quilt 'Little Egypt') the same methods of drafting are used, with the points being extended to fill in the required shape (Fig. 12).

These variations are simple to draft, but provide a challenge in piecing as each piece is shaped and sized differently – the only symmetrical pieces will be those inside the centre drafting circle.

OFF-CENTRE MARINER'S COMPASS

The off-centre block is simply a variation where the small drafting circle is shifted to a point within the larger circle other than its centre (Fig. 13). All calculations are made using the inner circle, but with the points radiating out to touch the outer circle in the same manner as Mariner's Compass with expanded perimeters.

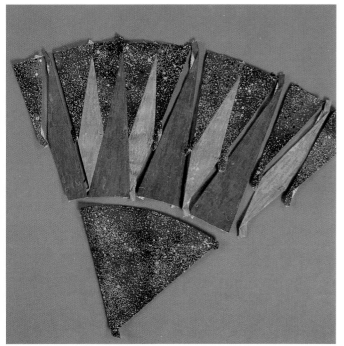

A segment ready to piece

An off-centre Mariner's Compass block

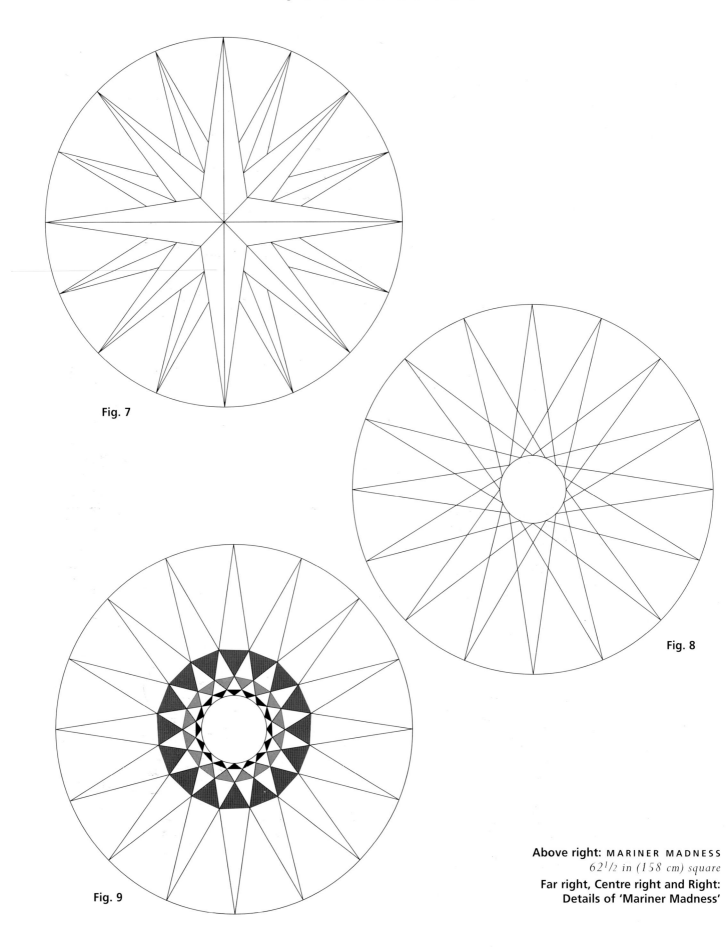

Fig. 7

Fig. 8

Fig. 9

Above right: MARINER MADNESS
$62^1/2$ in (158 cm) square
Far right, Centre right and Right:
Details of 'Mariner Madness'

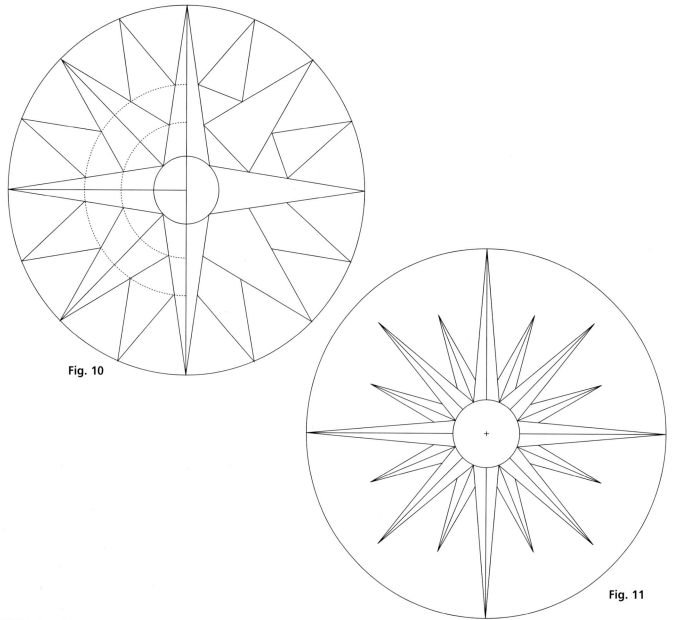

Fig. 10

Fig. 11

THE CENTRE CIRCLE

In some of the examples shown, the small drafting circle is left unpieced. This piece may be appliquéd in place after piecing the star points. However, you can also choose to fill this circle with a smaller, less detailed Mariner's Compass as in 'Any Port in a Storm' on page 62.

A WORD ON FABRIC SELECTION

For a dramatic block, look for strong contrast between the background fabric and the star points. Consider using placement prints or border stripe fabric for these points. A 'sky' print always seems a natural choice for the background fabric, as the Mariner's Compass block most resembles a star, but a Mariner's Compass is a dramatic block and looks just as good pieced in plaids, florals and small geometric prints. As with all patchwork, value is the key. Light fabrics opposed to dark will always give the most dramatic effect.

For a Split Mariner's Compass, consider using a wide stripe print instead of piecing the split. If you do wish to piece two different fabrics for a split compass block, join two strips of fabric together by machine, press the seam allowance open and iron on the freezer paper pattern, aligning the point with the centre of the seam.

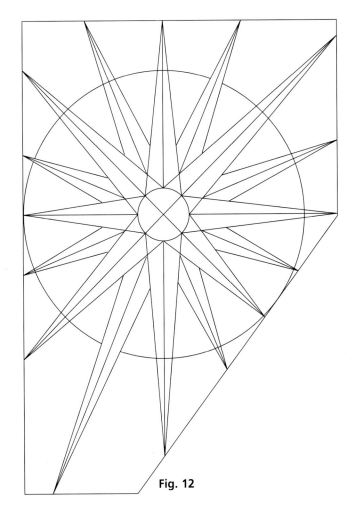

Fig. 12

PIECING

Because of the accuracy required by the Mariner's Compass block, I choose to hand-piece it, using a variation of the English paper-piecing method.

I enjoy hand-piecing, and this method eliminates the worry of seam allowances (even a small discrepancy will result in a wavy-edged or bubble-centred Mariner's Compass).

Make a master copy of your draft by choosing a letter for every fabric you plan to use, and marking each piece of the compass with its appropriate letter. Snip pieces of fabric and make a key in one corner of your master. Note that this method of piecing reverses the image.

Number each piece of the design, starting at the centre and moving outwards. Tape the master copy securely to freezer paper and trace the entire design (complete with all the letters and numbers) onto the dull side of the freezer paper. Cut the pieces out of the freezer paper pattern, dividing them into groups by their fabric letters. Set the iron to 'cotton' (dry) and iron the freezer paper pieces – shiny side down – onto the wrong side of the appropriate fabrics, leaving ⅝ in (1.5 cm) between the pieces. (**Note:** the grain line should 'radiate' throughout the Mariner's Compass as shown in figure 14).

Cut around each piece, leaving a seam allowance of ¼ in (6 mm). Baste the seam allowances over to the wrong side, except at the outer edge of the compass block. Don't worry about the tags that appear at the pointed ends of the pieces. These are easy to avoid while sewing and won't show on the wrong side. Make sure your folds are crisp and follow the papers as exactly as possible.

The master now becomes your map to follow in piecing the jigsaw back together. Place the pieces (wrong side up) on the master. Piece the background pieces to the smaller star points first, adding star points in order of size (Fig. 15).

PAPER-PIECING USING FREEZER PAPER

Cut the pattern pieces from freezer paper, leaving no seam allowances. Iron the pieces to the fabric, with the shiny side of the paper to the wrong side of the fabric, leaving a seam allowance between the pieces. Cut around the pieces, adding a ¼ in (6 mm) allowance. Baste the seam allowance over to the wrong side (dull side) of the paper, leaving the starting and ending knots on the right side. Hold the pieces with the right sides together, with the ends aligned, and sew them together with a small whip stitch, taking just a few threads from each piece with each stitch. Keep the stitches less than ¹/₁₆ in (1–2 mm) apart. When the whole block is joined together, appliqué it onto a background piece, and remove the basting and freezer paper.

Note: The thread for the whip stitch must match the fabric, as the tiny stitches will show on the right side of the finished block. The advantage of this method is that great accuracy in very complex blocks is relatively easy to achieve. However, because the seam allowance is split evenly to each side of the seam and the whip stitch forms a slightly ridged seam, hand-quilting on the seam line is difficult.

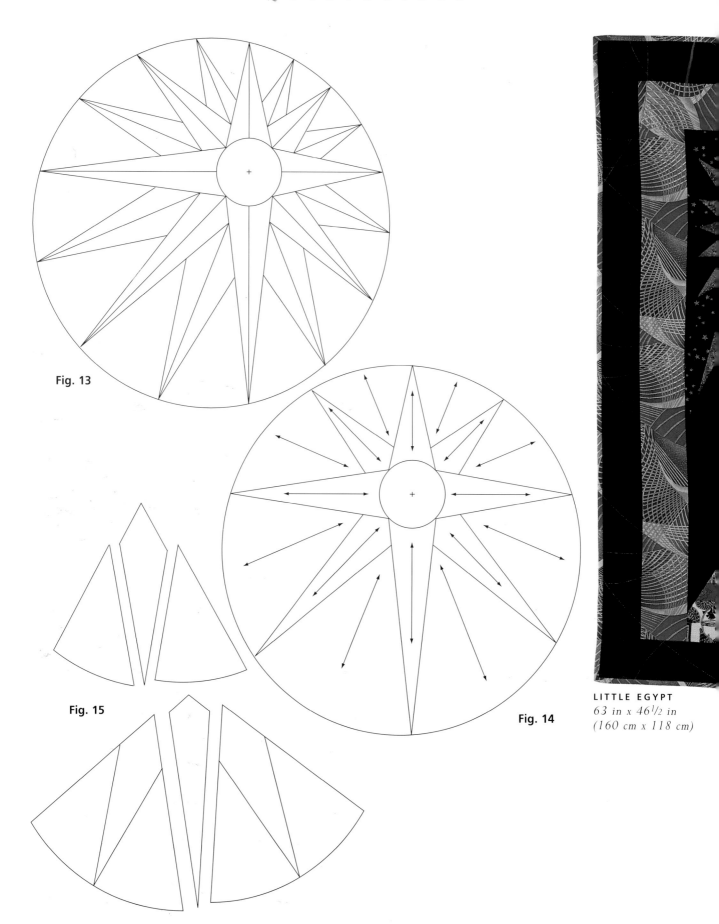

Fig. 13

Fig. 15

Fig. 14

LITTLE EGYPT
63 in x 46¹/₂ in
(160 cm x 118 cm)

Detail of 'Little Egypt'

CRAZY SKY CUBE
47 1/4 in x 48 in (120 cm x 122 cm)

CRAZY SKY CUBE

BARBARA MACEY

In the 1970s, an interest in embroidery and Op Art led me to develop my own version of traditional Log Cabin patchwork, which later evolved into a contemporary form of crazy patchwork. Today, I work in a bold, colourful, graphic style and, although abstract, my quilts often contain a reference to the Australian landscape.

The intriguing cube or tumbling block is a favourite traditional motif that also has an affinity with current patchwork trends. The motif came to Australia with the early immigrants and has become part of our quilting tradition. This contemporary version continues that tradition, connecting past and present. This quilt follows two wool quilts I made earlier; both were hexagon shapes without a background area.

This contemporary crazy patchwork quilt is graphic, yet pretty; challenging, but terrific fun to make, with great scope for adding your own ideas. The simple patchwork is machine-sewn to Pellon fleece or calico. Quilting is not strictly necessary so you can leave the patchwork as it is, or add embroidery or quilting, as you please.

You can easily adjust the size from a cushion, such as the one shown above, or a small wallhanging to a large bed quilt by increasing the number of blocks in the hexagon or by changing the size of the block. If you make the block larger or smaller, the size of the crazy patches should be enlarged or reduced also. For a really striking effect, repeat a cushion-sized hexagon all over your quilt or scatter small hexagons over the background.

PREPARATIONS

REQUIREMENTS

Note: These quantities will make a quilt 47 in x 48 in (118 cm x 122 cm). Wash all fabrics before use. Patchwork fabric: calculate the requirements on the basis that 1⅛ yd (1 m) of 45 in (115 cm) wide fabric makes seven 4¾ in x 9½ in (12 cm x 24 cm) blocks

Scraps or small lengths of fabric in lots of colours, in light, medium and dark values for the cube

5½ yd (5 m) of fabric for the background and binding

4 yd (3.5 m) of 36 in (90 cm) wide Pellon fleece, calico or lawn for the foundation

3¼ yd (3 m) of 36 in (90 cm) or 45 in (115 cm) wide fabric or piece several fabrics for the quilt backing

Machine sewing threads to match and contrast with the patchwork fabrics

Ruler and very sharp, soft lead pencil, 3B

Dressmaker's carbon paper in a dark colour (for calico foundations)

Thin cardboard

Sheet of thicker cardboard for the block templates

Pushpins, scissors, glass-headed pins, needles

Threads for hand-embroidery (optional)

Fusible webbing for appliqué (optional)

PREPARING MIRROR TEMPLATES

For a block 4¾ in x 9½ in (12 cm x 24 cm)

All the blocks are based on one parallelogram. The following construction method gives the correct angles with no fuss: cut a strip of thin cardboard ¾ in x 10¼ in (2 cm x 26 cm). Mark two dots, 9½ in (24 cm) apart. This strip works like a compass for drawing large circles. It can be lengthened or shortened for different-sized blocks. Make a hole through one dot, just large enough for the tip of a very sharp pencil. Push a pushpin through the other dot.

On the thicker cardboard, rule a line 20 in (50 cm) long close to one edge. Make a dot at the centre of the line and stick the pushpin, with the cardboard strip, through it. Place the tip of a pencil through the other hole in the strip and draw a semicircle. Use the compass strip to divide the semicircle into thirds, then rule lines to join the points to make a diamond. Divide it into two equal parallelograms (Fig. 1).

Cut out the parallelograms and label one Block A. Turn the other one over and label it Block B (Fig. 2).

PLANNING YOUR QUILT

The block diagram is given here at reduced size. You can make the cube exactly as shown or rearrange, reduce or extend it. Many variations are possible. Make several photocopies of your final design to try out the various value arrangements and colour schemes. Number all the blocks.

THE CUBE

You will need twelve Block A and twelve Block B.

For the block foundation: Cut the fleece or tear the calico into 6¼ in (16 cm) wide strips across the width of the fabric. Position the block template near one end of a strip of foundation fabric and draw around it. This outline is the seam line of the finished block. Repeat along the strip, leaving 2–2½ in (5–6 cm) between the block outlines. Cut the block foundations apart between the seam lines. For

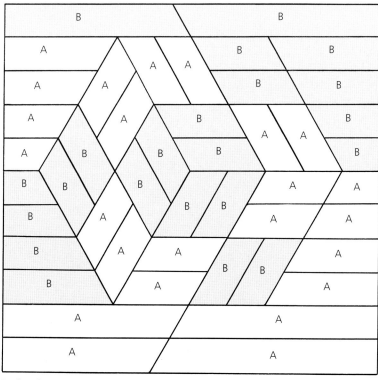

Quilt Diagram

economy, you can join foundation strips end to end by butting them together and sewing them with a medium zigzag stitch. These joins will not show through the patchwork.

There's potential for confusion with mirror blocks, so label them A and B now, using a safety pin to attach a small fabric label.

The seam lines you've drawn are on the right side of the foundation. For accurate seaming, you need them on the wrong side too. If you are using a calico foundation, place each block foundation right side up on dressmaker's carbon paper with the carbon side up. Trace once more over the seam lines, taking the lines right to the edge of the foundation. If you are using Pellon fleece, place the block foundation wrong side up on a light-coloured surface and trace once more over the seam lines.

PREPARING THE PATCHWORK FABRICS

The more variety in the fabrics the better. I've used plain fabrics because I wanted the machine stitches to be seen, but prints can also be used. Divide the fabrics into distinct light, medium and dark groups, rejecting any that don't look quite right anywhere.

Cut or tear the fabrics from selvage to selvage into strips from 3½ in (9 cm) to 5½ in (14 cm) wide. Press them thoroughly, then fold them length-wise and press them again. If you are using scraps, prepare them in the same way. Note that there is a double layer of patchwork fabric throughout.

CUTTING THE PATCHES

Cut a broad triangle from one of the wider folded strips and place it at the left-hand end of the block foundation, with the triangle fabric extending ³⁄₈ in (1 cm) into the seam allowance of the foundation fabric and pin as shown (Fig. 3).

Take another strip and place it so that the folded edge overlaps the raw edge of the triangle by about ³⁄₈ in (1 cm). Trim it to shape as shown, then pin it near the cut edge of the strip (Fig. 4).

Take a third strip and place it so that it overlaps the raw edges of the patchwork pieces already placed (Fig. 5). Place all the strips with the folded edge facing the first patch and vary the angle of each strip to

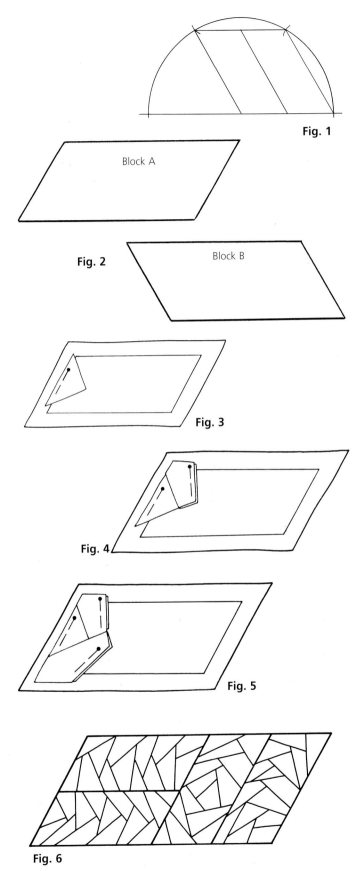

Fig. 1

Block A

Fig. 2

Block B

Fig. 3

Fig. 4

Fig. 5

Fig. 6

achieve a 'crazy' effect. Continue in this way until the block foundation is covered.

Start the patchwork at different ends of the block foundation for a more random effect (Fig. 6). You can begin the patchwork at any position on the block.

It's really a good idea to cut and place the patchwork fabric for the whole block before sewing, so you can gauge the effect, but, for now, cut and sew a little at a time, if you find that easier.

SEWING

Remove the pin from patch 2 and, keeping it in position, unfold it and sew along the crease, using a medium machine stitch (Fig. 7). Trim the seam allowance of patch 1 underneath, then fold patch 2 back into position and press. Use only a warm iron for pressing Pellon. Sew the remaining strips or patches to the foundation, trimming the seam allowances underneath and pressing carefully as you go.

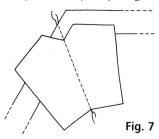

Fig. 7

Sew around the outside of the block, on the wrong side and 1/8 in (3 mm) outside the seam line. This line of stitching secures the edges of the patchwork and indicates the seam line position when you are quilting. Do not trim the foundation fabric at any stage.

EMBELLISHING

I worked simple geometric motifs in machine stitches, without the use of a hoop and before the blocks were joined. Use the machine's presser foot as a guide and count stitches for accuracy. It is easier to sew very accurately with a short stitch. Draw all the threads through to the back of the work as you go, then sew or tie them off.

Alternative ways to embellish the quilt include:
■ elaborate machine-embroidery;
■ hand-embroidery in contemporary or traditional crazy patchwork style to express interests, such as flora or fauna, memorabilia, sports, music etc;

■ signatures, embroidered or written with a fabric marker pen, for friendship quilts, but try out the pen on a scrap of your fabric first; and
■ appliqué, even if very simple, is very effective and quite easy, using a fusible webbing.

Embroidery can be bold or subtle and the colours should enhance the overall effect. Always experiment on scraps to be sure you are achieving the desired effect, before beginning on the blocks.

ASSEMBLING

Assemble the three large diamond shapes that make up the cube, but do not sew them together yet. Handling may have caused the long edges of some of the block foundations to become stretched. Pin the seams together at each end and gently 'dab' the seam with the iron to remove excess fullness. Press all the seams open as you work, but do not trim the seam allowances.

To match the seams accurately, first align them and place a pin at right angles to the fabric between the stitches of both seams. At this position, place a pin across the seam to be sewn and remove the original pin. Pin the rest of the seam. Sew to within 1/4 in (6 mm) of the matching seams, then raise the needle and lift the presser foot. Carefully move the work until the needle can be placed exactly in the position of the original pin. Lower the presser foot and sew back a few stitches, then forward carefully over the seam with the pin still in place.

BACKGROUND
PREPARING THE FOUNDATION

All the blocks in the background are extended or shortened versions of Block A or Block B. You can make a new set of templates using the measurements given in figure 8, however it is possible to get by with your original templates and a long ruler. Use a set square to draw the vertical lines on the template shown in figure 9.

Cut 6 1/4 in (16 cm) wide strips of foundation. For short blocks, draw around the template on the foundation, marking the position where the point of the parallelogram is to be cropped at a right angle. For larger blocks, draw around the template, extending

SCRAMBLE
48 in x 47¹/4 in
(122 cm x 120 cm)

QUILTSKILLS

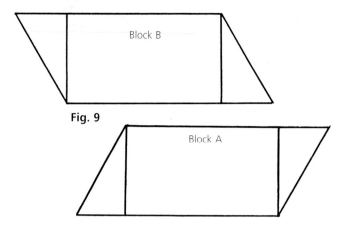

Fig. 9

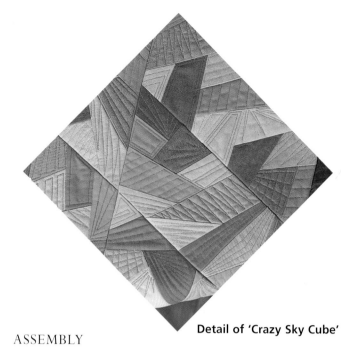

Detail of 'Crazy Sky Cube'

the long side(s) so the block ends in a right angle. For very long blocks, first draw one of the long seam lines the length of the foundation fabric as a guide for positioning the template. Mark the seam lines on the back of all the blocks.

PATCHWORK

There are eleven different blue fabrics in the background of 'Crazy Sky Cube', but you could use less than that, even one. Alternatively, you could have an entirely different background of landscape, sea, forest or cityscape.

Cut and sew the patchwork fabrics as for the cube. I have used irregular stars, birds and cube shapes in the quilting and have appliquéd the Southern Cross and Pointers in the dark sky areas.

Detail of 'Crazy Sky Cube'

ASSEMBLY

Figure 10 shows how the quilt is assembled in sections. Press the seams open as you go. Where three seams meet, do not sew into the seam allowance of the block. Press the seams open and fold the points of the block foundations so the seam allowances lie flat.

BACKING AND BINDING

For the binding, measure through the centre of the quilt and cut the binding to size. The bindings for the top and bottom should be the measured length plus the width of the side bindings plus ¾ in (2 cm) for turning the ends under. The finished width of the side bindings is ¾ in (2 cm); the finished width of the top and bottom bindings is 1¼ in (3 cm). Piece the binding, if necessary, to achieve the required length, then attach it to the quilt front only. The binding will be folded to the back of the quilt and secured by hand after the backing is in place.

Cut the quilt backing 1¼ in (3 cm) larger than the quilt. Tie the backing to the seam allowances of the patchwork, at intervals. Hand-baste the edges of the backing to the edges of the quilt.

HANGING THE QUILT

For hanging the quilt, attach a 4 in (10 cm) wide rod pocket at the top of the quilt back, securing the lower edge of the pocket to the seam allowances in four or five places.

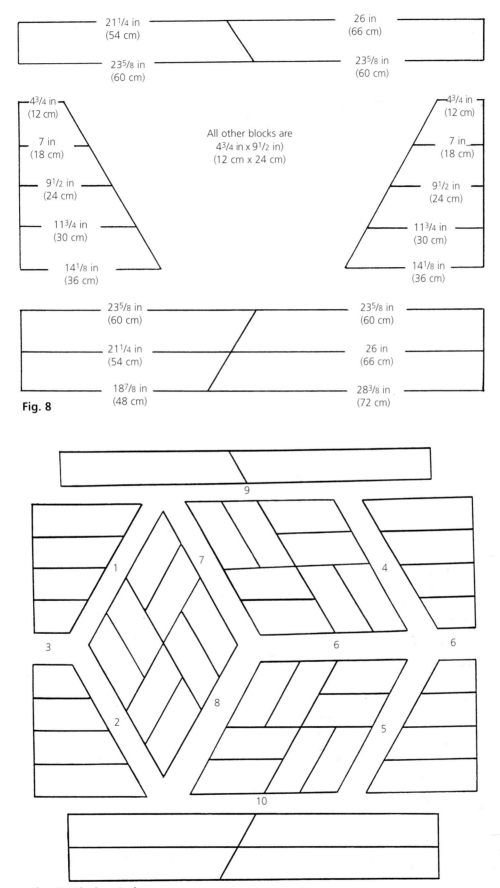

21¼ in
(54 cm)

26 in
(66 cm)

23⅝ in
(60 cm)

23⅝ in
(60 cm)

4¾ in
(12 cm)

4¾ in
(12 cm)

7 in
(18 cm)

7 in
(18 cm)

All other blocks are
4¾ in x 9½ in
(12 cm x 24 cm)

9½ in
(24 cm)

9½ in
(24 cm)

11¾ in
(30 cm)

11¾ in
(30 cm)

14⅛ in
(36 cm)

14⅛ in
(36 cm)

23⅝ in
(60 cm)

23⅝ in
(60 cm)

21¼ in
(54 cm)

26 in
(66 cm)

18⅞ in
(48 cm)

28⅜ in
(72 cm)

Fig. 8

Fig. 10 Piecing Order

NEPTUNE'S FANTASY
62 in (155 cm) square

BEYOND DRUNKARD'S PATH

SUSAN IACUONE

Historically speaking, compared to all the thousands of pieced patterns involving squares and triangles, there have been very few involving curves. This is due, in part, to a perception that curves are difficult to sew, particularly by machine. It is such a shame that many people feel this way, as the addition of a few curved lines increases design potential enormously, and in any case, curves are not difficult to sew.

BEGIN AT THE BEGINNING

We would all acknowledge that accuracy is vital to good results in quiltmaking, and would probably pay lip service to the necessity of accurate templates. However, how often have you traced off the templates at the end of the article or book assuming, firstly, that they're correct, and, secondly, that the seam allowance included actually corresponds to the one that you sew? Even in this age of specialised 1/4 in (6 mm) presser feet and movable needle position, there are no guarantees. It's still easy to sew a seam that's a smidgin off the theoretically perfect 1/4 in (6 mm). It may be possible to get away with the discrepancy when all the pieces are the same size, but it doesn't always work like that. In the case of curved seams, that smidgin can cause problems. Which is, I suspect, why curves often end up in the too-hard basket. Not any more!

So! The first step has to be to tailor your templates to the way that you sew. For this reason, the templates provided on page 87 DO NOT include the customary seam allowance – so you can't be tempted to just trace them off and skip this bit!

Begin by making an exact hand-drawn copy of each template on typing or writing paper. Be sure to leave at least ¾ in (2 cm) between each shape, so that they don't overlap once you have added the seam allowance.

Now over to your machine. Unthread the needle, set the machine for the longest stitch length, and use the foot and/or needle position that you consider to be ¼ in (6 mm). Place the paper copy of the template so that the seam line runs along the right side of the presser foot. Now proceed to sew around the shape with the unthreaded needle. Try to sew smoothly. When you've finished, you can 'play connect the dots' for a truly personalised perfect seam allowance. By now the penny should have dropped that this doesn't just apply to curves either! Just to satisfy your curiosity, why not check with a ruler or quilter's quarter to see how close you were to the customary seam allowance.

You will have noticed that the pattern pieces for this workshop have a small crosshatch at the mid-point of each curved edge. This should be copied and cut out as a shallow (less than ¼ in (6 mm)) notch on your plastic templates as an aid to matching up the pieces later, as you sew.

SEWING THE CURVE
The received wisdom about sewing curves by hand involves placing the outward curve (the quarter-circle or convex edge) to the back. Usually the same holds true in dressmaking, the reasoning being that the feed dogs will ease in the larger edge. So, when I started sewing Drunkard's Path units, that was how

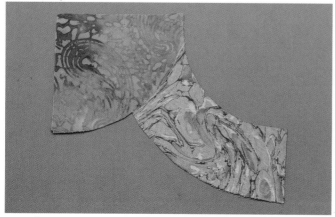

Detail A

I did it. In fact, I did it and taught it that way for years. Perhaps it was only bad luck that the ends of the seams were sometimes out by just a 'smidgin'. Then the penny dropped, and I decided to try it the other way round. Instant success! To begin, place the quarter-circle shape, with the right side down, on top of the next piece (Detail A). You may like to pin the end of the seam until you get the hang of working this way, so ease the end of the top piece around until it is aligned with the end of its mate and anchor with one pin.

Line up the leading edge of the two pieces and gently ease the top piece around, keeping the edges lined up as you sew. At this stage you can see if you are going to need to stretch the top piece ever so slightly to get the mid-point notches to match.

Once past the mid point, and with the end either pinned or just held so that it matches, it is easy to use the fingers of your right hand to ease the remainder as you sew. You will probably sew quite slowly to begin with and this may result in the line that you create being a little unsteady, but persevere for just a little while. As you build up a little more confidence and speed, you will find that it is easier to sew a beautifully smooth and accurate curved seam than you probably ever imagined.

DRUNKARD'S PATH VARIATIONS
The traditional Drunkard's Path unit has only two pieces and, even so, the number of traditional arrangements is reasonably varied (Fig. 1). If this traditional block is further subdivided, obviously the range of options will be extended. As the arc used in the basic block is usually drafted to intersect the outside of the block at a point one-quarter of the length of the side, it seems logical to parallel that arc, so that it divides the edge of the block at all the quarter points as shown in Block B (Fig. 3). A little further playing around showed me that combining some, or all, of these arcs created several other possibilities. My favourite, Block A, eliminates the very smallest curve so it's easier to sew but still looks interesting (Fig. 2). This block, combined with the basic Drunkard's Path, forms the basis for the design of 'Neptune's Fantasy' as well as part of 'Oilslick'.

NOW FOR THE FUN PART

How you approach the actual designing probably has a lot to do with whether you are a 'right brain' or a 'left brain' person. Some quilters get just as much pleasure from manipulating paper and pencils (or the computer screen) as they do from the actual making of the quilt. However, I fall into the other group. We're the ones that visualise better if we're working with the real thing. It's not a case of better or best, it's just what works for you.

I generally start by pulling out every fabric I own that fits in with whatever colour scheme I'm considering, and doing a bit of auditioning. I'm a great believer in instinct when it comes to colour and I buy what I like, when I see it, so that the palette is there to choose from when necessary. Generally, the only fabrics that get bought specifically for a particular project are the borders, backing and binding, and sometimes not even them.

It helps if you can be a little bit relaxed about 'wasting' fabric. Not huge amounts, of course, but you do need to feel free to discard things if they are not right. Personally, I start by cutting out a few of each shape from each of the fabrics that I think I'm going to use. I don't seem to use as many really light lights as I do the others, however, I will generally still cut a few of them out to get started. If you have a limited amount of a very special fabric, then you probably need to leave it intact for the time being.

Is your quilt going to include a full range of values from very light to very dark? Do you only want to go as far as the medium tones, no darks at all? Do you want to work only with lights and darks? No medium tones? Don't know? Well, use them all to start with and edit later.

Lay out your fabrics loosely from lights to darks. We are not aiming for the kind of perfect gradation of tone necessary for a colourwash approach, just an idea of what we have to work with. You may either choose to do this with all of your likely candidates, disregarding colour and focusing only on value (how dark they are), or you may prefer to grade each main colour family separately. Look at each of your fabric groupings. Do you have a full range of lights, mediums and darks? Are there any sudden jumps in value? You may want to consider using the reverse side of some of your fabrics, as I did quite a bit in 'Neptune's Fantasy'. This is an old trick, but it can be very effective.

When I began making 'Oilslick' in 1993, I had no particular colour strategy or image in mind. The previous experiments had used limited fabrics and although they proved to me that I could create interesting shapes with this set of blocks, the contrasts were stronger than I was happy with. I knew that I wanted something more subtle than the previous effort, but other than that, I had no fixed ideas – the proverbial blank canvas. What I did have was a wonderful group of lightweight furnishing fabrics in

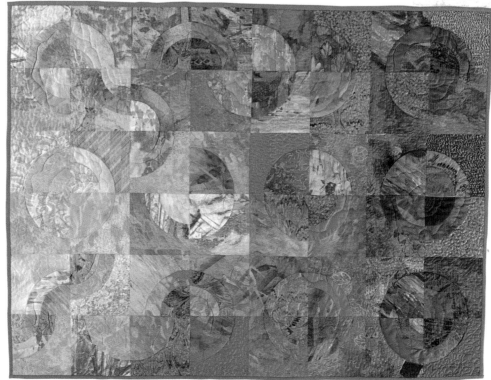

OILSLICK
35 1/2 in x 47 1/4 in (90 cm x 120 cm)

greens, browns, blues, mauves and greys with no florals or paisleys. They were all splodgy, painterly prints. Some of them were really quite ugly by themselves but, taken as a group, they had a wonderful opalescent sheen – not unlike the colours and patterns that oil drops leave on a wet road. Well, there was my image. A series of overlapping raindrops, randomly patterning an oily surface. Some of the drops would be full circles in isolation and others would have overlapped and broken up.

I knew that I wanted to go from darkish at one side of the quilt across to light on the other, as if a light was actually shining on the surface, and this meant that all of the blocks needed to be fairly low contrast. This actually proved to be an interesting problem, as some of my first choices were too strong and some of the later ones were so subtle that I might as well have saved myself the bother – you couldn't see where one fabric finished and the next began. I found that a door peephole from the hardware store was invaluable in this regard. Looking at a prospective block arrangement through the viewer quickly let me see when the effect was too bland or too strong.

Other than that, there really is little rhyme or reason as to which fabric goes in which position. Because of this approach, there is no pattern involved in the placing of light, medium and (relative) dark within each block. Some have the lightest as the large piece and some the darkest. Usually though, there is a flow across the block to the extent that light is next to medium next to dark, rather than say, medium next to dark, then jumping to light. Whatever looks good on the day, I guess.

In this instance I cut and sewed several blocks together from my darker fabrics, then laid them out to work out what was needed for the rest of the quilt. This way of working invariably leads to unpicking, but someone told me once that unpicking is good for the soul! Once you have your areas of colour and/or value mapped out, then you can decide on the actual orientation of your blocks. If you look at 'Oilslick', you will see that each group of four blocks on the darker side forms a circle and as you move across to the lighter edge, the blocks begin

to unravel and overlap like several drops of water falling in the same area. I didn't feel that this quilt needed a border.

When I started making 'Neptune's Fantasy', I wanted it to be quite different from 'Oilslick', so I made several design decisions before I started.

Firstly, the quilt needed to be 'square', although not symmetrical. The colours were to be stronger and, although I still wanted the light-to-dark movement, I wanted more definition within the block. I also decided to use a formal, more traditional arrangement of the blocks. As you can see, the same simple four-patch arrangement has been used throughout. There is, however, no real pattern as to which actual block was used where. I confined myself to only the basic block and to Block B, but then fitted them in where I liked.

In both cases, the background has been heavily machine-quilted, the random spiralling quilting on 'Oilslick' having been suggested by Nola Gibson. The arcs on 'Neptune's Fantasy' I decided to hand-quilt. It is also heavily beaded to suggest bubbles in the water. This one seemed to need a border to frame it, but I chose to keep it very simple. It was quite amazing how much darker the quilt became once I added the border, but I rather like the effect.

Detail of 'Oilslick'

86

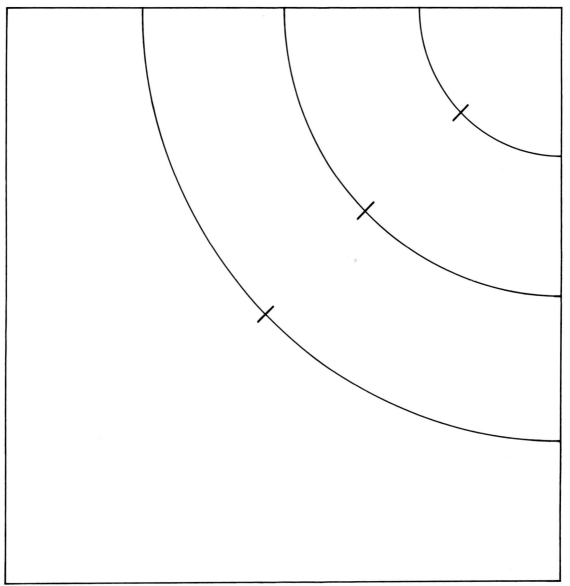

TEMPLATES

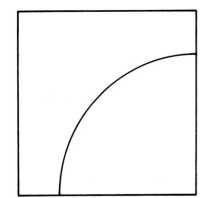

Fig. 1

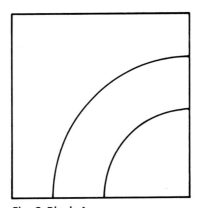

Fig. 2 Block A

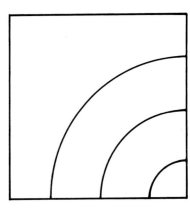

Fig. 3 Block B

PASTORAL CONSPECTUS
39¹/₂ in x 50 in (100 cm x 127 cm)

TEXTURE AND DIMENSION

Quilts in the Third Dimension

PAM HICKS

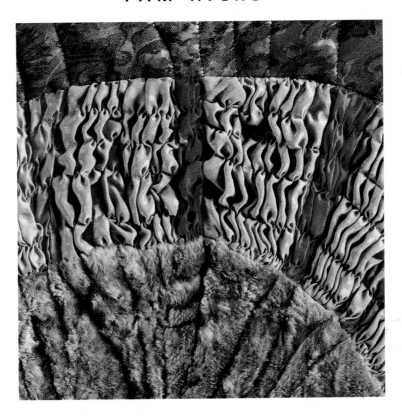

My love of textile arts has developed since I was very young. Today my work is evolving as I integrate skills and techniques and my experimentation with fabrics, threads and colour.

The brief I followed was to design and make a quilt by creatively introducing textural features and adding another dimension to the end result. The quilt was to be of aesthetic value, rather than functional, that is, a textile-art tactile medium, wall-hanging – rather than a bed quilt and one where colour and texture play a significant role in the development of the quilt design. I decided on the theme, using a mind map to generate and expand ideas. The inspiration for this quilt 'Pastoral Conspectus' came from aerial views taken whilst flying from the New South Wales Central Coast to the New South Wales North Coast. The theme then suggested its own colour scheme. The fabrics I chose to manipulate in the quilt are not those usually chosen for quiltmaking.

EXPERIMENTATION

The fabrics chosen for this project are manipulated by folding, cutting and sewing in numerous techniques, including traditional and non-traditional techniques, such as Seminole patchwork, ruching, trapunto, rouleaux, tucking and appliqué.

I envisaged fabrics being coloured by dyeing them in the microwave to produce fabrics that combine the full range of colours. Silk was chosen as the base fabric, as it is easily dyed, gives an even, good light- and wash-fast result, and produces a lovely lustre that enhances and reflects the other colours in the quilt. A large amount of fabric can be dyed in the one dye bath in a very short time.

Silk habutae is space-dyed in the microwave, using fibre-reactive dyes in the chosen colour run. Space dyeing is a simple method of obtaining variegated or monotone fabric in the required colour scheme.

It is important to be aware of the following safety guidelines when using powdered dyes:

- Use protective clothing, gloves and a dust mask.
- Good ventilation is essential.
- Do not use the equipment for any other purpose, once it is committed to the dyeing process.
- Do not drink, eat or smoke while using dyes.
- Thoroughly wash any equipment and the work space when the process is completed.

DESIGN

The quilt design is based on a theme developed through an understanding and application of the design elements: line, shape, direction, size, colour, tone and texture; and a consideration of design principles: emphasis, harmony, dominance, balance and rhythm. Colour and texture and the ambience they invoke are of particular importance in this project.

Begin by finding a suitable picture or photograph, or make an original sketch. Colour the sketch to give some idea of the final result. As I said earlier, this quilt was inspired by a picture taken while flying over the North Coast of New South Wales. The design lines were traced onto template plastic. A grid can be used to enlarge the design to the full size.

When an actual landscape is used, there is a feeling of the need to exactly replicate the scene. The quilt should be a personal interpretation and should be varied according to the quiltmaker's preferences: landforms can be moved kilometres, colours can be changed and additional design features can be incorporated in the final design.

THE MASTER PLAN

Using a permanent marker pen, copy the design lines onto a piece of non-woven interfacing the same size as the quilt (in this case, 39 in x 50 in (100 cm x 127 cm). Number each area of the design as shown on page 91.

On a second piece, draw the pattern blocks, marking each one with connecting notches, grain lines and identifying numbers, matching those on the master plan.

Now it is time to make colour choices, remembering that the colours need not be the same as in reality. Decide on the colour placement with the aid of small fabric swatches. When you are happy with your choices, glue the swatches to the master plan.

The next step is to decide on which textural effects are required and where they will be placed on the design to create the most effective and interesting result. The design principles listed earlier are important to consider here.

TECHNIQUES

SEMINOLE PIECING

Sample 1 Cut satin fabric into 1½ in (4 cm) widths, then cut these into 1½ in (4 cm) and 2½ in (6.5 cm) lengths.

Use both sides of the fabric to gain a shiny and a matte combination, then alternate shiny and matte fabric, and long and short pieces. Sew them together in strips using a ¼ in (6 mm) seam allowance. Press the seams to one side.

Next, piece these strips together, offsetting each strip so the patches do not match up (Fig. 1).

Sample 2 Cut strips 1½ in (4 cm) wide from two different-toned fabrics. Sew them together, alternating fabrics, with the right sides facing and using a ¼ in (6 mm) seam allowance (Fig. 2). Press the

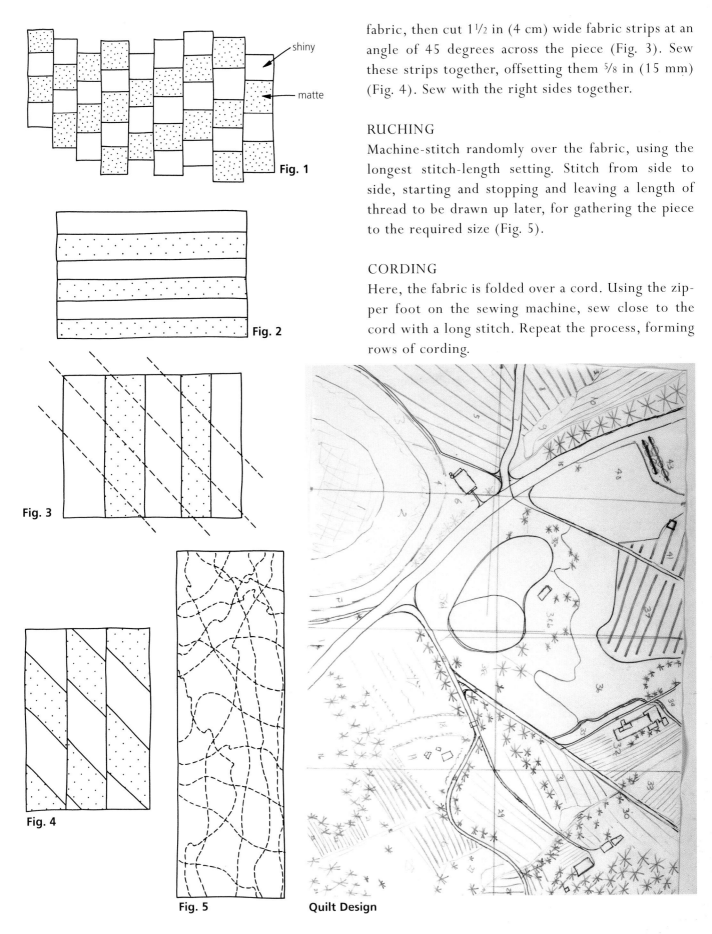

fabric, then cut 1½ in (4 cm) wide fabric strips at an angle of 45 degrees across the piece (Fig. 3). Sew these strips together, offsetting them ⅝ in (15 mm) (Fig. 4). Sew with the right sides together.

RUCHING
Machine-stitch randomly over the fabric, using the longest stitch-length setting. Stitch from side to side, starting and stopping and leaving a length of thread to be drawn up later, for gathering the piece to the required size (Fig. 5).

CORDING
Here, the fabric is folded over a cord. Using the zipper foot on the sewing machine, sew close to the cord with a long stitch. Repeat the process, forming rows of cording.

shiny

matte

Fig. 1

Fig. 2

Fig. 3

Fig. 4

Fig. 5

Quilt Design

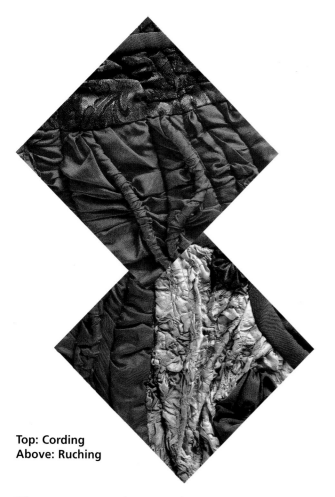

Top: Cording
Above: Ruching

These rows can be straight or curved, parallel or random. The cord can be the same thickness, or a variety of thicknesses can be used.

Finally, the cord is pulled up to create the gathered effect. The amount of gathering will change depending on how tightly or loosely it is pulled (Fig. 7).

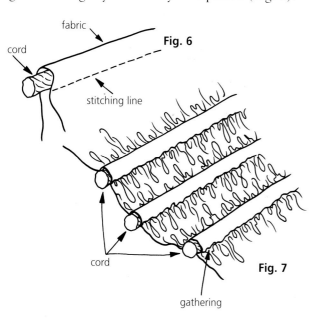

YO-YOS

Cut a number of circles from several different fabrics, each approximately 3 in (8 cm) in diameter. Vary the size of the circles to gain added interest.

Thread the needle with matching sewing thread, turn under a 1/8 in (2 mm) hem and, using a small running stitch, sew around the outside edge of each circle. Draw up the stitching as tightly as possible.

It is necessary to firmly secure this stitching at the start and at the end. Use a few stitches worked from side to side, ending with a back stitch to secure the circle closed.

Yo-yos can be attached to the quilt by hand- or machine-stitching.

BLOOMING LAYERS

Pin five layers of fabric together, arranged in order from the lightest to the darkest, or as desired. Machine-stitch in rows or a grid pattern, through all the layers. The lines of stitching should be up to 5/8 in (15 mm) apart (Fig. 8).

Cut through the top four layers with sharp scissors in the centre of two rows of stitching, taking care not to cut the bottom layer (Fig. 9).

Machine-washing will assist the 'blooming' process, but be sure that your fabrics are wash-fast

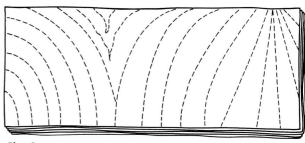

Fig. 8

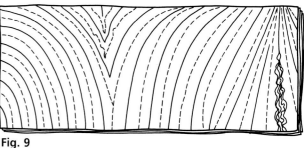

Fig. 9

so that the dye does not run and spoil your work.

Rub a ruler back and forth along the cut edges to create and exaggerate the ragged effect.

TUCKING AND DARTS

Fold the fabric over with the wrong sides together and sew a tuck on the right side of the fabric. Place these tucks randomly, varying them in length and width (Fig. 10).

TRAPUNTO

First back the fabric, then sew a pattern with enclosed shapes (Fig. 11). From the back of the piece and using sharp scissors, slit through the backing in the middle of the sewn shape (Fig. 12). Fill the space with a polyester filling and slipstitch the opening closed. This technique produces raised areas for added texture (Fig. 13).

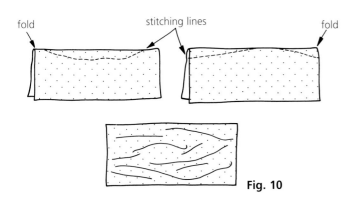

Fig. 10

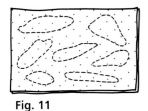

Fig. 11

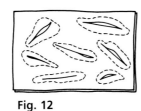

Fig. 12

Fig. 13

SHIRRING

Set the sewing machine to a large stitch and wind shirring elastic onto the bobbin. Using only a slight pressure on the presser foot, stitch randomly over a piece of fabric stretched in a frame. You may need to adjust the top tension.

It is important not to release the fabric from the frame until the stitching is completed, because the elastic will cause the fabric to retract, creating difficulties later when the work is reframed.

When the stitching is completed, pin the piece onto a calico piece, cut to the required shape. Be sure to pin closely because the shirred piece must be stretched into the correct shape. Stitch over any large puffy sections, adding more or less stitching, depending on the effect required. The more densely a piece is stitched, the less dimension is achieved.

SMOCKING

Several lightweight fabrics can be pieced together, then fed through a smocking pleater, set up with threads that blend with the fabrics. The pleater set-up can be varied according to the number of rows and the space between the rows.

When they emerge from the pleater, the fabrics are tightly and evenly gathered. The gathers can be arranged according to the shape of the pattern piece. By moving them, the area can be sparsely or densely gathered and worked around curves.

The pleated fabrics are then stitched to a calico base, through all the layers, leaving the gathering threads in place. These threads must be tied off prior to the piece being stitched to the base fabric.

ENHANCEMENTS

Braids, beads and other decorations can also be added to the quilt surface. They can be stitched on by hand or by machine. These enhancements create subtle gradations that play with light, forming reflections and shadows. This encourages the eye to explore and discover the quilt's focal point and beyond. They energise the fabrics, colours and textures of the quilt to complete a unique visual statement.

CONSTRUCTION

ASSEMBLY

After the theme is conceptualised; the resources obtained, and the design, techniques and colours planned, it is time to construct the quilt.

Begin by washing and ironing all the fabrics. Dye all the silk habutae as planned.

All the textural techniques are constructed in 'slab' pieces, then cut into the field pattern blocks. The blocks are cut to include a ¼ in (6 mm) seam allowance. Ensure that matching notches are cut on all the pieces.

The quilt is crazy-pieced together onto a calico base to which the iron-on batting has been attached. Once each block is made, it is pinned, then machined into place, with the right sides together, starting at one corner and working out and down. This process quilts as you go.

At times, it is necessary to slipstitch sections by hand when you 'machine yourself into a corner'. For example, one side of the road is machined, while the other side is slipstitched into place.

Remember to clip into the curves so that they will sit neatly when they are pieced together. Trim and grade seams to reduce the bulk in the seam allowances.

Buildings and houses are appliquéd by turning under a small seam allowance and machine-stitching them into place. The yo-yos and ruched trees are also machine-stitched onto the quilt.

Any additional quilting or enhancement can be added by hand or by machine, depending on your individual design and personal preference.

BACKING AND BORDERS

The quilt is completed by straightening the sides and ensuring that the corners are square. To do this, measure diagonally from corner to corner, and if these two measurements are the same, the quilt is square. If not, use a T-square to adjust accordingly.

The backing fabric must coordinate with the quilt top, as it will form a mock binding, folded over to the front and becoming a part of the front of the quilt. Cut the backing 3 in (8 cm) larger than the quilt top. Place all the layers on a flat surface, pin

them together, then thoroughly baste, ensuring that the layers will not move independently.

The backing is machine-stitched to the quilt 2¼ in (6 cm) from the quilt edge, through all the layers. At each corner, fold the backing to meet the corner of the quilt top. Cut off the corner (Fig. 14). Fold the trimmed corner onto the quilt top (Fig. 15). Turn under a ¾ in (2 cm) hem on the backing and fold it to the front, meeting with the stitching line and completing the mitred corners. The entire self-binding is then slipstitched with matching thread. Note that the needle only picks up a few threads from the quilt top and does not go through to the back.

HANGING SLEEVE

Finally, make and attach a hanging sleeve by cutting a piece of backing fabric that is as long as the quilt is wide and 8 in (20 cm) wide. Turn under a ⅝ in (1 cm) hem on the short sides and sew with the machine. Centre the sleeve on the back of the quilt 4 in (10 cm) from the quilt top. Turn under a ¾ in (1.5 cm) hem, then pin and slipstitch the sleeve to the back of the quilt. Repeat the process for the other side of the hanging sleeve, attaching it 5 in (12 cm) from the other side. The sleeve is sewn onto the back with some slack which allows room for the hanging rod.

Hang up your quilt and stand back to admire your wonderful quilt creation!

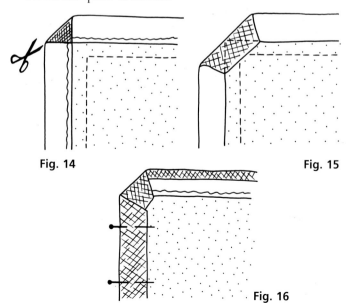

Fig. 14   Fig. 15

Fig. 16

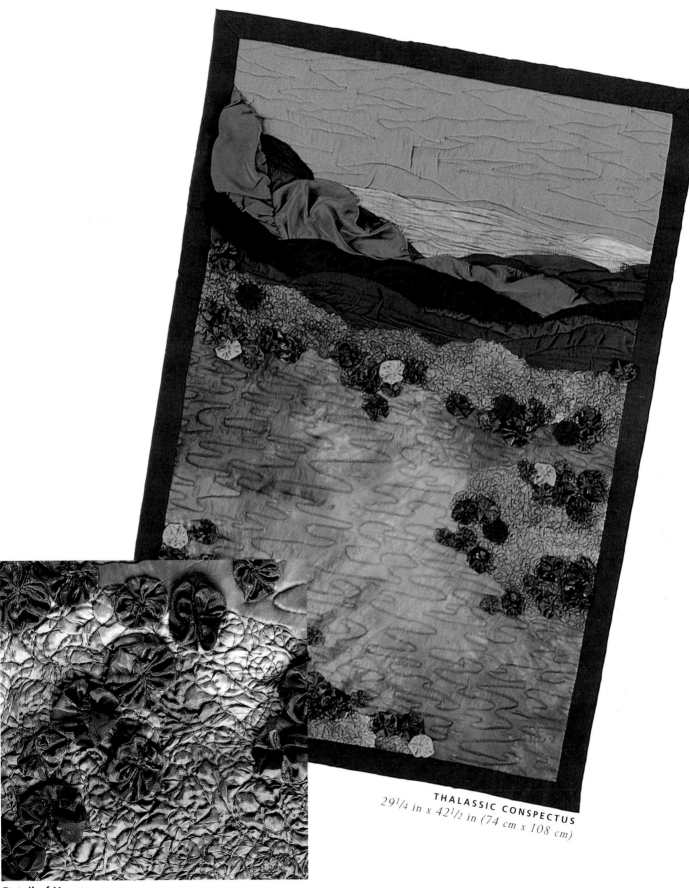

THALASSIC CONSPECTUS
29¹/4 in x 42¹/2 in (74 cm x 108 cm)

Detail of Yo-yos

THE TUTORS

Trudy Billingsley
119 Collins Road
St Ives NSW 2075
Tel: 02 9449 4141
Workshops in fabric manipulation and surface collage, creative garment construction and embellishment, shadow work and transparent overlay, fantasy costumes

Eileen Campbell
104 Derby Street
Kew Vic. 3101
Tel: 03 9853 7248
Workshops in machine skills involving appliqué, embroidery and quilting

Pam Hicks
PO Box 942
Newcastle NSW 2300
Workshops in patchwork, machine-quilting, colour and design, hand- and machine-embroidery, appliqué, printing, dyeing, spinning, wearable and fantasy clothing

Barbara Macey
117 Lawrence Road
Mount Waverley Vic. 3149
Tel: 03 9803 1359
E-mail: jmacey@melbpc.org.au
Workshops in foundation-piecing, including designing off-beat Log Cabin and contemporary crazy patchwork

Cynthia Morgan
1A Crees Parade
Caloundra Qld 4551
Tel: 075 491 2098
Workshops in dyeing for cottons and natural fibres, disperse dyeing for synthetics, quilts from nature, textures

Wendy Saclier
27 Nelson Place
Curtin ACT 2605
Workshops in Victorian crazy patchwork, pieced pictures, beginners to advanced traditional patchwork and quilting

Christa Sanders
14 MacDonald Place
Spence ACT 2615
Tel: 02 6258 2945
Workshops in original design, colour and symbols

Alison Schwabe
3 Doric Street
Shelley WA 6148
Tel: 09 9354 8148
Fax: 09 9457 7011
Basic design principles, pattern-free and template-free construction, irregular shapes, innovative hand- and machine-quilting, simple fabric printing techniques

Adina Sullivan
23 William Street
South Grafton NSW 2461
Tel: 066 42 4683
Workshops in design and colour application, rotary cutting, machine-piecing, hand-piecing, hand-embroidery and machine-quilting

Sue Wademan
PO Box 337
Springwood NSW 2777
Tel: 047 513638
Fax: 02 9954 9264
Workshops in design-focused areas in machine skills and collage, and motivational lectures

Susan N. Iacuone
9 Cerutty Way
Wantina South Vic 3152
Tel: 03 9801 5542
Specialises in one-of-a-kind quilts, Drunkard's Path, Mystery quilts, Japanese design, Celtic design, Tesselations, colourwash quilts, and Log Cabin variations

EDITORIAL
Managing Editor: Judy Poulos
Editorial Assistant: Ella Martin
Editorial Coordinator: Margaret Kelly

PHOTOGRAPHY
Andrew Payne

ILLUSTRATION
Lesley Griffith

PRODUCTION AND DESIGN
Production Manager: Anna Maguire
Production Coordinator: Meredith Johnston
Layout: Lulu Dougherty
Cover Design/Design Manager: Drew Buckmaster
Concept Design: Michele Withers

Published by That Patchwork Place
20205 144th Avenue NE
Woodinville, WA 98072-8478
An imprint of Martingale & Company
www.patchwork.com
By arrangement with J.B. Fairfax Press Pty Limited
A.C.N. 003 738 430

Formatted by J.B. Fairfax Press Pty Limited

Printed by Toppan Printing Co. Singapore
© J.B. Fairfax Press Pty Limited 1998
JBFP 472US
QUILTSKILLS
Workshops from The Quilters' Guild Australia
ISBN 1 56477 213 6